SPECIAL COMMEMORATIVE BOOK

ONE TEAM, ONE HEARTBEAT

Matthew Emmons/USA TODAY Sports

Safety Grant Delpit admires the national championship trophy after LSU defeated Clemson at the Mercedes-Benz Superdome. (Mark J. Rebilas/USA TODAY Sports)

LSU
8

This book is available in quantity at special discounts for your group or organization.

For further information, contact:

Triumph Books LLC
814 North Franklin Street
Chicago, Illinois 60610
Phone: (312) 337-0747
www.triumphbooks.com

Printed in U.S.A.
ISBN: 978-1-62937-703-2

The Daily Advertiser/USA TODAY Network
Brett Blackledge / Executive Editor
Heidi Venable / Sports editor
Glenn Guilbeau / LSU beat reporter
Photos: USA TODAY Sports
Contributing reporters: Roy Lang III, Andrew J. Yawn and John Marcase

Content packaged by Mojo Media, Inc.
Joe Funk: Editor
Jason Hinman: Creative Director

Front cover photo by John David Mercer/USA TODAY Sports
Back cover photo by Matthew Emmons/USA TODAY Sports

CONTENTS

FOREWORD

By Bunnie Cannon

I have heard the 1958 Fighting Tigers' 11-0 national championship football season called "magical" and "perfect." It was the first time in 22 years that LSU won the Southeastern Conference championship; the first time in 50 years it had gone undefeated. The 1958 Tigers were a special, close-knit team, the likes of which have not been seen again at LSU until this season.

The similarities between the two teams are borderline cosmic. Each team started the season under fairly new head coaches. Paul Dietzel was entering his fourth season in 1958. Ed Orgeron was also entering his fourth season, if you count 2016 when he was interim head coach. Each team held a super power, a special player who unified their squads. In 1958, it was my dad, tailback Billy Cannon. In 2019, it was quarterback Joe Burrow. Both players would win the coveted Heisman Trophy, and as a result become iconic heroes at LSU, in Louisiana and nationally.

Interestingly, Burrow visited LSU to consider a graduate transfer from Ohio State just a week before Cannon passed away peacefully on May 20, 2018, at age 80. Did the famed No. 20 know Burrow was coming? Probably so, because he knew most things related to LSU football before they happened. On that day, he passed the torch and went home.

My dad always wanted to share the Heisman Trophy with another Tiger. On several occasions he thought he would — quarterback Bert Jones in 1972, quarterback Tommy Hodson in 1988 and 1989, defensive back Tyrann Mathieu in 2011 and tailback Leonard Fournette in 2015. When he was introduced as "LSU's only Heisman trophy winner," his response was always, "Yet!" Yet is now.

There would have been no one happier than my dad that Burrow now shares the honor of winning the Heisman. Burrow is an incredibly gifted, hard-working young man with an incredibly grounded family and support system. There is no one more deserving to carry the torch for LSU.

No. 20 would have been so happy to see the accolades of the 2019 Tigers.

Football was such a big part of my dad's life, especially in his golden years. He was a master of the game, and he studied it. He would be amazed at how well the 2019 Tigers' talent has developed — the speed and agility of Ja'Marr Chase and Justin Jefferson at wide receiver, the power and perseverance of Clyde Edwards-Helaire at tailback, or the passion of Breiden Fehoko and Rashard Lawrence on the defensive line. I wish my dad were here so I could have heard his commentary on this magnificent team.

Another factor that both teams seem to have is the camaraderie between players and coaches. Cannon would have been so supportive and proud of Coach Orgeron, offensive coordinator Steve Ensminger and the entire coaching staff for all they have done to work with this amazing team.

Orgeron has overcome adversity in his career and has finally acquired his dream job at LSU. He had the foresight to promote Ensminger and to keep defensive coordinator Dave Aranda. Ensminger has flourished as offensive coordinator and helped recruit former Saints assistant coach Joe Brady to become the pass game coordinator. My dad would have loved to see LSU's Dream Team of coaches come alive and a passing offense he always believed LSU should have.

If he were still here, I can picture him in the Moran's

The LSU Tigers gather around senior Stephen Sullivan for the pre-game huddle in New Orleans. (Stephen Lew/USA TODAY Sports)

suite in Tiger Stadium, sitting in seat No. 9 — the seat he sat in every game for about eight years — with his steely blue eyes watching the game intently, a wad of chewing tobacco in his cheek while holding a spit cup. Cutting those eyes briefly and glancing over saying, "It just doesn't get much better than this!"

The icing on the cake? What team did the 1958 LSU national champions beat, 7-0, to finish their perfect season on Jan. 1, 1959, in the Sugar Bowl in New Orleans? Clemson. Coincidence?

The players, coaches and scores were different, but the heart is the same.

One Team, One Heartbeat. … Or, make that Two Teams, One Heartbeat.

FOREVER LSU! ■

— **Bunnie Cannon**
Executive Director, Tiger Athletic Foundation
LSU B.A. 1992 & LSU M.S. 1997

INTRODUCTION

By Glenn Guilbeau

Once upon a time, a Cajun man was literally "Born on the Bayou" in Larose, Louisiana, and took a route as meandering as the Mississippi River itself to his dream job — a national championship as LSU's head football coach.

And on the night of Jan. 13, 2020, he paddled his proverbial pirogue up the Mighty Mississippi, which curves just blocks from the Mercedes-Benz Superdome, where his Fighting Tigers of LSU defeated Clemson to win the national championship and finish off the greatest season in program history at 15-0.

The only previous undefeated national champion at LSU was the 1958 team that finished 11-0 after a 7-0 win over Clemson in the Sugar Bowl in Tulane Stadium in New Orleans on Jan. 1, 1959.

"There's no way I could have written a better script," LSU coach Ed Orgeron said. "No way."

And he did it with a roster full of fellow Cajuns, Louisianans, and converted Louisianans, such as a quarterback from The Plains, Ohio, named Joe Burrow — aka Jeaux Burreaux.

"I'll always feel like I'm from Louisiana. This place and its people embrace you like one of their own," said Burrow, a transfer from Ohio State.

And they embrace you back after you leave like a prodigal son, which is what Orgeron did at age 18 as a freshman at LSU. He quit the Tigers football team in August 1979 after signing as a top lineman out of South Lafourche High in Galliano, where he was recruited by Alabama coach Bear Bryant.

"Yeah, there was unfinished business when I left LSU," Orgeron said as his return reached its climax in the Crescent City — just 62 miles from his birthplace. "I didn't give myself a chance to compete at the highest level like I should have as a player. So I was a little disappointed in myself. I wanted to get the chance to come back to LSU and prove myself."

His golden opportunity came on Sept. 25, 2016 — the day coach Les Miles was fired after an 18-13 loss at Auburn that dropped the Tigers to 2-2 after being ranked No. 5 to start the season. He was named interim head coach and answered with a 5-2 record, got the permanent job two days after a 54-39 Thanksgiving Night win at Texas A&M in the regular season finale, and won the Citrus Bowl over No. 15 Louisville to finish 6-2.

But a 9-4 season followed with the same offensive problems that plagued Miles.

Orgeron reacted swiftly, firing his hand-picked offensive coordinator Matt Canada, and returning old friend Steve Ensminger to the job. LSU went 10-3 in 2018, marking its first double-digit win season since 2013.

Then he made the bold move that jettisoned LSU into the era of aerial offense that had spread throughout the nation for years as the Tigers clung to a more conservative, outdated scheme. Orgeron hired 29-year-old lower offensive assistant Joe Brady from the New Orleans Saints. Brady had all of two seasons as a full-time assistant in college football.

Paired with Burrow under the watchful eye of Ensminger and using talented wide receivers Justin Jefferson, Biletnikoff winner Ja'Marr Chase and Terrace Marshall Jr., along with tight end Thaddeus Moss and tailback Clyde Edwards-Helaire, Brady was the finishing touch on a perfect storm at LSU that produced the greatest offense in school history, arguably the best in Southeastern Conference and NCAA history.

LSU won its last five games before the clash with

A view from the top of the Mercedes-Benz Superdome as Joe Burrow takes a snap in the third quarter of the College Football Playoff national championship game against Clemson (James Lang/USA TODAY Sports)

Clemson by an average of 32 points and never trailed in the second half since Auburn took a 13-10 lead in the third quarter on Oct. 26 before going on to lose 23-20. LSU entered their final game No. 1 in the nation in total offense with 564.2 yards a game, No. 1 in scoring with 48.9 points a game, and with Burrow No. 1 in passing efficiency at 204.6 on 371-of-478 passing for a SEC record 5,208 yards and a SEC record 55 touchdowns.

"No, I couldn't imagine the offense would be this good," Orgeron said. "And it's not about the records. It's about the wins, but it's been phenomenal — the most prolific offense in SEC history. Nobody ever dreamed of that at the beginning of the year."

Others saw it coming, too, though not quite with the dominance and pizazz with which LSU has dominated opponent after opponent.

"I knew how Coach O was going to take his talent and look at our talent and figure out how he was going to put us in the best positions and hire the best coaches to put those guys in the best positions," LSU junior safety JaCoby Stevens said.

But Stevens did not predict the explosion of offense from Burrow.

"No, I didn't foresee that," he said. "I mean, I'm not an oracle. But I'm glad he came to LSU. He helped my odds."

Ensminger, a senior quarterback at LSU in 1979 when Orgeron quit and returned home to Larose, did foresee Orgeron's success when he became interim coach. Ensminger was an assistant with Orgeron at McNeese in 1985 when both were still in their 20s.

"I've known him for a long time," Ensminger said. "And the only thing I do know about Coach O is he's a tough son of a bitch. I knew it when he got the job."

And the big Cajun man proved it.

"It has been a storybook season," he said.

And LSU lived happily ever after?

The End. ■

CFP NATIONAL CHAMPIONSHIP

LSU 42, CLEMSON 25

JANUARY 13, 2020 • NEW ORLEANS, LOUISIANA

BEST. SEASON. EVER.

LSU completes perfect season with win over Clemson for national title

By Glenn Guilbeau

Picture Perfect.

More than 12 minutes remained in the national championship game Monday night, and LSU quarterback Joe Burrow suddenly directed the LSU band and flashed a million dollar smile.

It was already over.

No. 1 LSU completed the greatest season in its football history at 15-0 with a dominating, stylish, 42-25 victory over defending national champion and previously 29-0 Clemson in front of 76,885 at the Mercedes-Benz Superdome.

"This was what I wanted to do since the time I was 5 years old," Burrow said on the field after accepting the Offensive Most Valuable Player award for the game. Then he thanked everyone he could think of, including the chefs at LSU's dining hall.

"This is for everybody," LSU coach Ed Orgeron said. "One team, one heartbeat, baby!"

It was the Tigers' fourth national championship.

Burrow's fourth touchdown pass — a 4-yard toss to tight end Thaddeus Moss for a 35-25 lead with 5:13 left in the third quarter — was his 59th of 2019-20 and broke the NCAA record for touchdown passes in a season held by Hawaii's Colt Brennan at 58 since 2006.

A graduate transfer senior from Ohio State, Burrow finished 31-of-49 passing for 463 yards with six touchdowns in all, as he also ran for a 3-yard score in the second quarter.

Ed Orgeron hoists the national championship trophy following his team's 42-25 victory over the defending national champions Clemson. (Stephen Lew/USA TODAY Sports)

LSU
2020
SEC
LSU
22
6

Tight end Thaddeus Moss (81) celebrates with wide receiver Justin Jefferson (2) after scoring a touchdown in the second quarter. (Mark J. Rebilas/USA TODAY Sports)

Tailback Clyde Edwards-Helaire rushed for 110 yards on 16 carries while catching five passes for 54 yards. Wide receiver Ja'Marr Chase caught nine passes for 221 yards and two touchdowns, while wide receiver Justin Jefferson caught nine passes for 106 yards.

Clemson quarterback Trevor Lawson completed only 18-of-37 passes for 234 yards and zero touchdowns against LSU defensive coordinator Dave Aranda's unit. Tailback Travis Etiene of Jennings gained 78 yards on 15 carries.

LSU outgained Clemson 622 yards to 394.

But the Tigers had found themselves down 17-7 with 10:38 to play in the first half after a 36-yard end around for a touchdown by Clemson wide receiver Tee Higgins.

This after the Tigers managed just 90 yards and three first downs in the first quarter and did not cross their own 12-yard line on their first two possessions. Clemson had 160 yards and eight first downs.

Opposite: Ja'Marr Chase makes a catch for one of his two touchdowns. Above: Thaddeus Moss (81) and wide receiver Justin Jefferson (2) celebrate in the endzone. (Mark J. Rebilas/ USA TODAY Sports)

For Louisiana native Ed Orgeron, the Tigers' national championship is the culmination of a long coaching journey that finally brought him home. (Mark J. Rebilas/USA TODAY Sports)

LSU
7
2020
ACC
5

But then LSU's offense arrived in the Big Easy and began to wilt the vaunted Clemson defense that entered the game leading the nation in fewest points allowed with 11.5 points a game, in pass defense with 151.5 yards allowed a game, and second in total defense with 264.1 yards allowed a game.

On their next three possessions following the 17-7 deficit, the Tigers moved in the following fashion:

- 75 yards in five plays over 1:21 ... Touchdown on a 3-yard run by Burrow.
- 87 yards in six plays over 2:03 ... Touchdown on a 14-yard pass from Burrow to Chase.
- 95 yards in 11 plays over 3:28 ... Touchdown on a 6-yard pass from Burrow to tight end Thaddeus Moss.

LSU suddenly led 28-17, and Clemson (14-1) never led again. ■

Opposite: Grant Delpit nearly makes an interception during the first quarter against Clemson. (Matthew Emmons/USA TODAY Sports) Above: Clemson running back Travis Etienne (9) is tackled by LSU defensive end Neil Farrell Jr. (92) in the second quarter. (Mark J. Rebilas/USA TODAY Sports)

LEGENDARY

Move over Billy Cannon, Joe Burrow will be No. 1 on LSU's Mount Rushmore

By Roy Lang III

Joe Burrow left purple-and-gold tire tracks the size of a monster truck on Trevor Lawrence's No. 16 at the Mercedes-Benz Superdome. This wasn't a knock on the play of Clemson's quarterback, but rather the destruction LSU's hero has levied against the competition all season.

Burrow, again, made one of the nation's top defenses look sophomoric and his counterpart impotent.

With 463 yards passing and six touchdowns (five through the air) in No. 1 LSU's 42-25 victory against No. 3 Clemson, Burrow put an emphatic conclusion to the best season by a college football quarterback — including a record 60 passing touchdowns — and cemented his Tigers' 2020 campaign as the greatest in the history of the game.

"(Burrow) is great," Lawrence said of Offensive MVP Burrow. "He's unbelievable."

Heisman jinx my keister.

LSU captured its fourth national championship and left an incredible path of destruction. The Tigers, who amassed nearly every major individual award available for 2019, defeated seven teams ranked in the top 10 at the time of the matchups this season, including blowout victories against Nos. 4 (Georgia), 4 (Oklahoma), and 3 (Clemson) to finish.

The Tigers broke the all-time NCAA scoring record with 726 points this season (Florida State, 723 points in 2013).

Meanwhile, Lawrence lost his first game as a college quarterback. He completed 18-of-37 passes for 234 yards and added a rushing touchdown.

Neither an injury scare nor horrendous early field position would deny Burrow another mind-boggling performance.

"It's amazing to be a part of history," LSU sophomore receiver Terrace Marshall Jr. said.

Media inquired about a potential rib injury, Burrow brushed it off, although he was clearly laboring in the waning moments of the first half Monday.

"There's been so many people that have come into this, from people that have helped me along my journey from Ohio, Louisiana, everywhere," Burrow said. "We couldn't have done it with a better group of guys, not just football players but great, great men that I just feel blessed to be a part of this."

Burrow's time in Baton Rouge is over, but his legend will grow forever. Billy Cannon's place as No. 1 on LSU's Mount Rushmore is tenuous at best. It's hard to imagine another Tiger will ever, or should ever, wear No. 9.

The grainy footage of the 1950s has helped Ole Miss fans question whether Cannon stepped out of bounds on the most talked about play in Tigers history — his punt return touchdown on Halloween in 1959. Fast forward to the 21st century, where Burrow's achievements — and highlights — will forever be crystal clear.

Joe Burrow cradles the national championship trophy after an MVP performance, one for the history books. (Mark J. Rebilas/USA TODAY Sports)

LSU
2020
LSU
9
2020

"I love Dr. Cannon, will always love Dr. Cannon for what he did for LSU, but in the moment it's hard not to have (Burrow) No. 1 in any pecking order," said former LSU running back Jacob Hester. "We'll give them 1A and 1B — how bout that?"

Said Burrow: "I don't know about the whole hero thing, but I know this national championship will be remembered for a long time in Louisiana. To do it in New Orleans is even more special." ■

Opposite: Joe Burrow managed an incredible 463 passing yards in LSU's championship performance. Above: Burrow greets fellow quarterback Trevor Lawrence after the game. (Mark J. Rebilas/USA TODAY Sports)

Joe Burrow dives into the endzone for a second-quarter touchdown. (Mark J. Rebilas/USA TODAY Sports)

9

UNBREAKABLE

LSU's 2019 season has been so perfect, it seems as if everyone is pinching themselves

By Glenn Guilbeau • December 27, 2019

LSU's revolution of 2019 was televised.

It started on Sept. 7 on ABC during prime time from Austin, Texas, where the No. 6 Tigers exploded for 573 yards behind a slinging senior transfer quarterback named Joe Burrow, who completed 31-of-39 passes for 471 yards — second most in a game in LSU history — and four touchdowns in a 45-38 win over No. 9 Texas.

For the first time in LSU history, three LSU wide receivers — Justin Jefferson, Ja'Marr Chase and Terrace Marshall Jr. — each had 100 yards receiving.

Burrow did the queen's wave to the Longhorn fans late in the game with the outcome no longer in doubt as LSU Brexited from its old guard football ways and into the Texas night.

And nothing has been the same since.

"You're not used to that one," Burrow said wryly after the game, because he knew it was coming. He said it over the summer, and people laughed.

"I think we're going to score a lot of points," he said at the Manning Passing Academy in Thibodaux last June. "And I don't think a lot of people are used to LSU scoring 40, 50, 60 points a game. If we do what we need to do, we can be one of the best offenses in the country."

True. True. True. And true.

Oh, and Burrow won the Heisman Trophy two weeks ago after being a 200-to-1 pick to win it over the summer. He did not predict that one.

"I thought we'd be good in the passing game," said LSU coach Ed Orgeron, who brought in Saints assistant coach Joe Brady to be his pass game coordinator and install a real spread, no-huddle attack for the first time at LSU. "But not this good."

Brady has been the talk of the nation right along with Burrow. Brady, only 30, became the first non-coordinator to win the Frank Broyles Award that goes to the nation's best assistant coach.

"It's just made a world of difference to see it on TV," Orgeron said. "Every time you turn on the TV, they're talking about LSU's offense."

LSU backed up Burrow's boasts immediately as it won its season opener, 55-3, over Georgia Southern, beat Texas, 45-38, in game two, beat Northwestern State, 65-14, and Vanderbilt, 66-38, as Burrow broke the school record of five touchdown passes in a game with six. As recently as 2010, LSU quarterback Jordan Jefferson threw just seven touchdown passes all season, and he started 13 games and threw for 1,411 yards in an 11-2 campaign.

LSU hit half of 100 three-straight times to end the regular season — 58-37 at Ole Miss, 56-20 over Arkansas, and 50-7 over Texas A&M.

Burrow was wrong about the overall offense. It was not one of the best in the country. It is the best in the country in total offense with 554.4 yards a game. And Burrow is No. 1 in the nation in completion percentage with an NCAA record .779 (342-of-439) and in touchdown passes with a Southeastern Conference season record 48. His 4,715 passing yards is an SEC season record as he broke the mark of 4,275

LSU's Mike the Tiger mascot points during the first half of the Tigers' 66-38 win over Vanderbilt on September 21. (Christopher Hanewinckel/USA TODAY Sports)

SEC
LSU
1

held by Kentucky's Tim Couch since 1998 two games ago.

LSU's previous record holder for passing yards in a season was Rohan Davey with 3,347 in 2001.

Burrow is also the No. 1 active quarterback in the nation in passing efficiency at 201.5 with Alabama's injured Tua Tagovailoa still leading at 206.9.

"I thought Joe Burrow was the difference in the ball game," Texas coach Tom Herman said after the LSU loss. "Just really accurate, and really aggressive."

Herman recruited Burrow out of Athens, Ohio, in 2014-15 when Herman was Ohio State's offensive coordinator.

"He fit some balls into some really tight windows," Herman said. "Really accurate downfield. He's going to have a heck of a year."

True.

Going into the Peach Bowl on Saturday in the national semifinal at Atlanta's Mercedes-Benz Stadium, Burrow is tied with Oklahoma quarterback Jalen Hurts in points responsible for with 308.

Chase, meanwhile, won the Biletnikoff Award that goes to the nation's top receiver, as he is No. 1 in the nation in receiving yards on the season with 1,498 and in receiving yards per game with 124.8. His 18 touchdowns tied the SEC record set by Florida's Reidel Anthony in 1996.

LSU is the first SEC team in history to have a 4,000-yard passer, two 1,000-yard receivers in Chase and Justin Jefferson (1,207 on 88 catches, 14 TDs), and a 1,000-yard rusher in tailback Clyde Edwards-Helaire (1,291 yards on 197 carries, 16 TDs).

Edwards-Helaire, though, is questionable for the Oklahoma game with a hamstring injury suffered on Dec. 17 in practice.

Others saw LSU revolutionizing its brand of football long before Sept. 7.

"In the spring, the offense was really getting good," LSU senior defensive end Rashard Lawrence said.

Then over the summer, the whole team was at the facility on its own for workouts.

"And they were gettin' after it," Lawrence said. "I've been here four years, and usually you'll have people in separate groups here and there. But this was the first year where the whole team was up here on a Saturday, and it wasn't mandatory. And we were all here competing, but just enjoying ourselves."

Suddenly, LSU was 8-0 and No. 1 in the nation with three top 10 wins — No. 9 Texas, No. 7 Florida, 42-28, and No. 9 Auburn, 23-20.

But next was Alabama, which was also 8-0 and also No. 1 in a poll and was 8-0 against LSU beginning with the national championship game in the 2011 season.

"We knew we had to beat Alabama," Lawrence said. "We knew we had to win the SEC championship to really have everything fall into place."

LSU never trailed and led 33-13 at the half before Alabama came back and drew within a touchdown three times in the second half before succumbing, 46-41.

"We should've won by more," Burrow said.

The Tigers had finally broken through the pressure barrier, as former LSU athletic director Skip Bertman used to say when he was coaching the Tigers' baseball team to five national championships.

"That day is surreal," Edwards-Helaire said of the Bama win. "From the moment we woke up, everything just felt defined and magnetized for some reason. Didn't know why. It didn't feel like any other day when I woke up. It just felt like it was in slow motion from the moment I woke up and from that point all the way throughout the game and to the end of the game."

LSU's 2019 season has been surreal from the beginning to now. No LSU team in history has won more major, national awards. In addition to Burrow's Heisman, Brady's Broyles Award, and Chase's Biletnikoff, Orgeron has won two national coach of the year awards, safety Grant Delpit won the Thorpe Award for the nation's best defensive back, and the offensive line won the Joe Moore Award for the nation's best offensive line.

Burrow won the school's first Heisman in 60 years and also picked up the Maxwell Award and the Walter Camp Award for the nation's best player. The program's best season ever at 15-0 with a national title is there for the Tigers.

And the team has been virtually void of any off-field discipline issues, which plagued LSU's last 13-0 team in 2011. Senior outside linebacker Michael Divinity has missed much of the season on suspension, and other players missed a game here and there for team rules violations.

"There's not a lot of drama," Orgeron said. "Guys taking care of their business. Guys coming to work early, doing their work, practicing hard, going home, resting. It's a close team.

LSU fans traveled and filled the stands at Vanderbilt Stadium. Behind a record-breaking passing game led by Heisman Trophy-winning quarterback Joe Burrow, the Tigers kept their fans cheering throughout the 2019 season. (Christopher Hanewinckel/USA TODAY Sports)

It's what we wanted."

The only thing missing is the school's first national championship since the 2007 season and fourth overall. Two more wins would give LSU its greatest championship season at 15-0.

"You look at the banners around here, and there's one more banner that needs to be hung," senior defensive end Breiden Fehoko said. "Everybody is trying to do something that hasn't been done in a while here."

LSU is a Hollywood overnight success — years in the making from the firing of Coach Les Miles in 2016 when Orgeron took over, to a rough start in 2017 with a 37-7 loss at Mississippi State and a 24-21 upset loss to 20-point underdog Troy.

Orgeron fired offensive coordinator Matt Canada less than a year after hiring him as his first savior of the offense. LSU improved from 9-4 in 2017 by only one win to 10-3 in 2018, but with a 29-0 loss to Alabama. That loss, though, is what convinced Orgeron he needed to go to the spread offense.

"Well, then hire somebody who knows it," offensive coordinator Steve Ensminger told him. And one of the best co-coordinator relationships in college football screen history was born.

"It took us three years to get here," Orgeron said the day before the SEC title game. "There was a couple of good decisions and a couple of decisions that weren't so good. But thankfully, they gave me the time to get it right, and I feel like we're on the right track now."

Lawrence, who signed in 2016 out of Neville High in Monroe, feels it, too.

"A lot of us were here for that Troy loss," he said. "This all started a long time ago. Through the years, through the good and the bad. But this definitely is a team that's unbreakable." ■

LSU
9
LSU
9
Riddell

LSU 55, GEORGIA SOUTHERN 3

AUGUST 31, 2019 • BATON ROUGE, LOUISIANA

LSU OFFENSE OPENS IN MIDSEASON FORM

Burrow ties school record for single-game TD passes

By Glenn Guilbeau

Wow! What a passing offense at LSU of all places.

For a minute there, I thought LSU had hired Tom Herman after all.

Or better yet, Jimbo Fisher.

But no, it was the new passing game coordinator phenom "Mighty" Joe Brady, the 29-year-old wunderkind who studied at Sean Payton's headphones with the New Orleans Saints the last two seasons.

Not a bad opening night for Brady, whose pass offense put up 350 yards with quarterback Joe Burrow throwing a school record-tying five touchdown passes in but one half during No. 6 LSU's 55-3 win over Georgia Southern in the season opener Saturday night at Tiger Stadium.

"I thought Joe was on fire," said LSU coach Ed Orgeron, who got his job permanently when LSU couldn't quite hire Herman or Fisher after the 2016 regular season. "He was hitting his helmet against the wall before the game. He was ready to go. He's a gamer. Thank God we have him."

Orgeron appears to have the makings of a passing offense the likes of which LSU has not seen on a consistent basis since Fisher was the Tigers' offensive coordinator from 2000-06.

"You know we have a great scheme," Orgeron said. "There were receivers who were open. Great concepts going on out there tonight."

Later, he delivered the quote of the night. "The scheme is a lot better this year. We have answers," he said.

Imagine that. In other words, in the past, if something in the passing game did not work, LSU was pretty much done. There was no Plan B. See two shutouts in three years to Alabama.

"We know we can throw the ball," Orgeron said. "What we saw tonight is what we've been looking for at practice. I'm very pleased with our offense."

No fewer than 14 players caught at least one pass for the Tigers, including three by tight ends.

By halftime, the Tigers led 42-3, Burrow had already thrown for 253 yards on 20-of-24 passing and the five touchdowns, and they apparently had barely worked up a sweat.

Look what is already on Joe Brady's resume:

- The 42 points were the most by LSU in the first half of an opener at least since 1945. The statistics do not reach before that.
- The 55 points were the second most by LSU in an opener since 1933 and most since a 55-3 over Texas El Paso in the 1997 opener.
- The 21-0 lead in the first quarter was the Tigers' largest advantage in an opening period since they led Kent State, 21-0, in 2013, which was the last year LSU had a good passing offense.

LSU unveiled its new passing offense in grand fashion as Joe Burrow threw for five touchdowns in the first half of LSU's 55-3 season-opening win over Georgia Southern. (Derick E. Hingle/USA TODAY Sports)

BAKER
31
LSU
9

- The Tigers opened a game with five straight scoring drives for the first time since a 56-0 win over Sam Houston State in 2014.

A notoriously slow-starting team on offense for years, LSU looked in mid-season form — of a good season like 2003 or 2007.

"A lot of teams expect to have rust in the first game," Burrow said after leaving early in the third quarter, Tua Tagovailoa style, with 278 yards on 23-of-27 passing and seven scoring drives. "But there is no rust to be had."

LSU looked fast, lean, and mean on both sides of the ball. That's not news on defense, but it definitely is on offense.

"Whenever you call a play and have an answer to every coverage and every blitz they can give you, you know you are going to be successful," Burrow said. "Whatever I see against a defense now, I have an answer every play."

Now, now, this was Georgia Southern. No. 10 Texas will be much better on defense.

"There are still 11 more games that we have to prove it," Burrow said. "We are going to keep building on this thing and make it even better."

Hopefully, LSU did not empty the playbook.

"We showed everything we got," Burrow cracked. "All of it. Make sure you write that."

LSU's playbook, which Orgeron said was only skimmed, was clearly a new edition available online. No huddles, fast pace. Of the Tigers' seven touchdown drives, six of them lasted 2:24 or less, and five featured six plays or less.

"More wide receiver sets, RPOs (run-pass options), hurry up," Georgia Southern coach Chad Lunsford marveled.

Stuff just not seen around these parts.

LSU's offense is not in Kansas anymore.

Les Miles is. ■

Clyde Edwards-Helaire led a balanced LSU rushing attack that gained 122 yards and scored two touchdowns against Georgia Southern. (Derick E. Hingle/USA TODAY Sports)

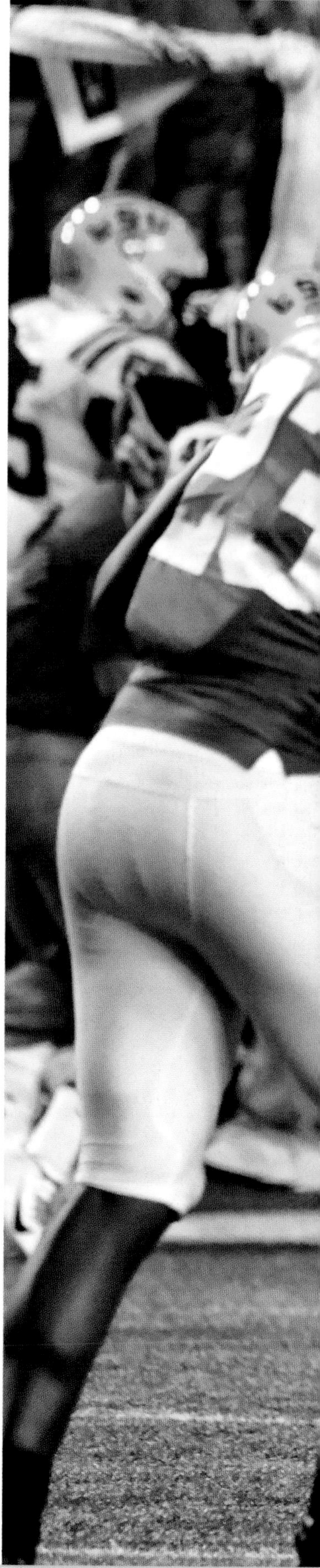

LSU 45, TEXAS 38

SEPTEMBER 7, 2019 • AUSTIN, TEXAS

TEXAS HOLD 'EM

LSU out-duels Texas in awe-inspiring display

By Glenn Guilbeau

LSU and Texas threw one down Saturday night.

But the No. 6 Tigers threw a few more and outlasted the No. 9 Longhorns in an Austin aerial showcase, 45-38, that surely pleased an ABC national TV audience as well as 98,763 on hand — and at the edge of their seats — at Texas Memorial Stadium.

Quarterback Joe Burrow completed 31-of-39 passes for 471 yards — second most in LSU history — and four touchdowns, while Texas quarterback Sam Ehlinger hit 31-of-47 for 401 yards and four touchdowns.

"You're not used to that one," Burrow said smiling.

"What a game," LSU coach Ed Orgeron said. "What a game! What a night for college football!"

Burrow finally turned the lights out on the stubborn Longhorns (1-1) with a 61-yard touchdown pass to wide receiver Justin Jefferson with 2:27 to go for a commanding, 43-31 lead that grew to 45-31 when Burrow hit wide receiver Ja'Marr Chase on a two-point conversion pass.

Before the touchdown, Burrow faced a third-and-17, but he stepped up in the pocket, leaned away from a teammate blocking, and let it fly for Jefferson, who caught it in stride and sprinted the remaining 40 yards for the score.

The Tigers, unlike in years gone by, were not trying to run out the clock. They weren't trying to pass out the clock either.

"We knew we were going to have to score again. We said, '40, and we'll win,'" Burrow said.

"That kid's a baller," Orgeron said of Burrow. "He lives for the moment. This is a tough place, and he got it done."

Joe Burrow celebrates after completing a 61-yard touchdown pass to Justin Jefferson to seal LSU's win over No. 9 Texas in Austin. Burrow threw for four touchdowns. (Scott Wachter/USA TODAY Sports)

BURROW
9

LSU

Only quarterback Rohan Davey has thrown for more yards in LSU history with 528 in a 35-21 win at Alabama in 2001.

"I thought Joe Burrow was the difference in the ballgame," said Texas coach Tom Herman, who recruited Burrow out of Athens, Ohio, in 2014-15 when Herman was Ohio State's offensive coordinator. "Just really accurate, and really aggressive. He fit some balls into some really tight windows. Really accurate downfield. He's going to have a heck of a year."

For the first time in LSU history, the Tigers had three 100-yard receivers as Jefferson caught nine for 163 yards with three touchdowns, Chase had eight for 147 yards and Terrace Marshall Jr. added six catches for 123 and a touchdown.

LSU (2-0) collected a huge victory toward its early College Football Playoff hopes in the first top 10 pairing of the young season.

"That was a hell of a college football game," Herman said. "A hell of an atmosphere." ■

Opposite: Receiver Ja'Marr Chase maneuvers past a Texas defender. Chase had eight catches for 147 yards. (Scott Wachter/USA TODAY Sports) Above: LSU center Lloyd Cushenberry (79) prepares to snap the ball in the second half against the Texas Longhorns. (Scott Wachter/USA TODAY Sports)

79
4
150

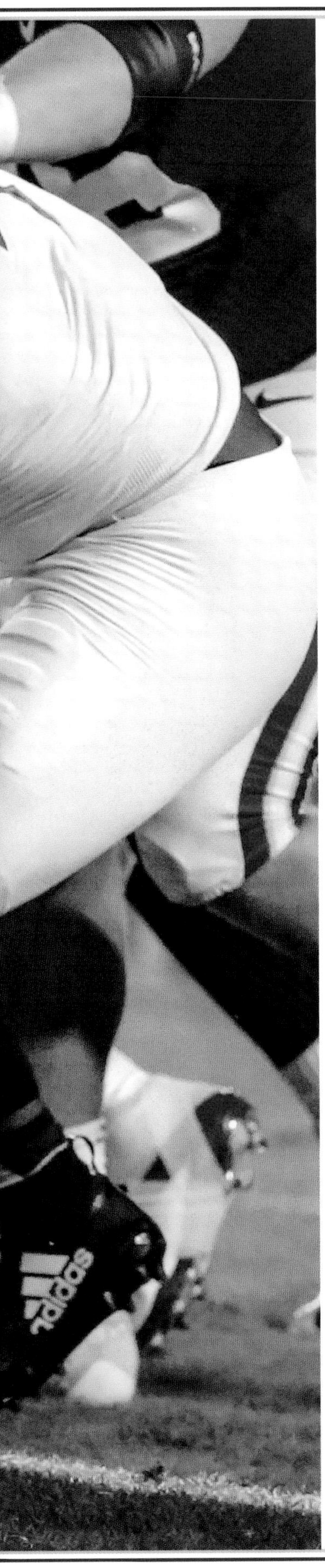

LSU 65, NORTHWESTERN STATE 14

SEPTEMBER 14, 2019 • BATON ROUGE, LOUISIANA

FROM HANGOVER TO BLOWOUT

LSU recovers from slow start, routs Northwestern State

By Glenn Guilbeau

LSU's defense needs to go to the hurry-up, and get better fast.

The No. 5 Tigers' opponent descended, but their defense still looked like it was playing Texas' high-flying offense from last week at times as LSU struggled to contain 51-point underdog Northwestern State early before rolling to a 65-14 win Saturday night at Tiger Stadium.

LSU (3-0) saw its defense pick up where it left off last week when it had to outscore the No. 9 Longhorns, 45-38.

"In the first quarter, I was a little mad," LSU coach Ed Orgeron said. "We had to face some adversity, and we did. We needed a game like this."

LSU's defense threw a shutout in the second half and eventually won by the point spread, but it found itself down 7-3 in the first quarter after the Demons (0-3) drove 75 yards in eight plays for a touchdown on a 17-yard pass from quarterback Shelton Eppler to wide receiver Quan Shorts. Northwestern State followed that with another 75-yard drive in six plays to cut the Tigers' lead to 17-14 with 5:38 to go before halftime.

Northwestern State, which lost to Midwestern State of Wichita Falls, Texas, by 33-7 a week ago and 42-20 to Tennessee-Martin in its season opener, actually outgained LSU, 114 yards to 102 in the first quarter. Eppler was 9-of-12 passing for 96 yards in the opening period.

LSU running back John Emery Jr. reaches across the goal line to score a touchdown, giving LSU a 44-14 third quarter lead over Northwestern State. (Derick E. Hingle/USA TODAY Sports)

"Some of the plays we made in the first half, we didn't make in the second half," Northwestern State coach Brad Laird said. "The atmosphere wasn't too big for this football team."

The Demons did not punt in the first quarter and had only two by the half.

"We need to take this as a learning experience and come out punching," said linebacker Jacob Phillips, who led the Tigers with eight tackles. "Don't come out with our hands down. But we shut them out in the second half."

The Tigers finally established some order on a 70-yard drive in six plays late in the first half to take a 24-14 lead on a 3-yard touchdown run by tailback Clyde Edwards-Helaire, but it could have been closer. Northwestern State kicker Scotty Roblow missed a 34-yard field goal with 35 seconds left in the half to keep LSU up by 10.

Quarterback Joe Burrow left the game in the third quarter after completing 21-of-24 passes for 373 yards with two touchdowns (both to wide receiver Terrace Marshall Jr., for 14 and 6 yards) and an interception while rushing seven times for 30 yards and a touchdown.

Myles Brennan replaced Burrow and finished 8-of-9 passing for 115 yards.

The Tigers finally started putting up the big score expected when freshman tailback John Emery Jr. scored on a 4-yard run for a 44-14 lead with 6:26 to go in the third quarter.

LSU made it 51-14 late in the third quarter on a 1-yard touchdown run by freshman tailback Tyrion Davis-Price. True freshman Trey Palmer returned a punt 54 yards for a touchdown and a 58-14 lead with 7:22 to play in the game.

Then the Tigers added one more touchdown on a 2-yard touchdown run by Davis-Price with 2:12 to play for the 65-14 final. ■

LSU backup quarterback Myles Brennan completed eight of nine passes for 115 yards in relief of Joe Burrow during LSU's 65-14 win over Northwestern State. (Derick E. Hingle/USA TODAY Sports)

LSU
DEMONS
McNEELY
95
15
SU

LSU
LSU

HEAD COACH

ED ORGERON

Like the Rougarou, the infamous swamp monster of Louisiana lore, LSU head coach has seemingly snuck up on the college football world

By Andrew J. Yawn • December 6, 2019

The further south you head on Highway 1, the more tales of him you hear.

Eyes widen as they tell how he was born and raised in this corner of southeast Louisiana among the shrimp boats and oil canals. How he'd devour everything in sight and how, even at a young age, he was as large as a black bear with strength to match. You'd know he was near when your ear was tickled by his unmistakable growl.

This isn't the story of the Rougarou, the fabled werewolf said to prowl these marshes and snatch children wandering out past their bedtime. But like the infamous swamp monster of Louisiana lore, LSU head coach Ed Orgeron has seemingly snuck up on a college football world that more than once stopped believing in him.

Now Larose is telling a new legend of the man they call Bébé, the native son leading the undefeated Tigers toward a playoff push and a potential fairy tale ending for a rough-and-tumble region that could use something to smile about.

"Oh the people are so proud," said the coach's mother, Coco Orgeron. "When the tears come down from his eyes, we all cry, because we know what it feels like as a Cajun that we elevated ourselves to show people we can do things."

LSU is no stranger to success. The team hasn't posted a losing season since 1999. Previous head coaches Nick Saban and Les Miles each lifted the Tigers to championship heights.

Orgeron's No. 2 Tigers have gotten back to those winning ways, ripping off 12 straight wins en route to an SEC Championship clash with No. 4 Georgia. But there's a sense in the Bayou State that this season is more than a yet-to-be-defeated team gunning for a chance at glory.

It's about being led there by a man who used to shovel shrimp in southernmost Louisiana's Lafourche Parish. It's a journey defined by second chances for a man taught coaching from a litany of Hall of Famers and recruiting by watching his grandfather coax customers to his vegetable stand. And it's validation for fans who know if he wasn't stalking the sidelines of Death Valley, he'd be with them in the stands rooting for LSU all the same.

"You can't get more Louisiana than Coach O, and you can't get more Louisiana than Bayou Lafourche," said former New Orleans Saints quarterback Bobby Hebert, who grew up down the road from Orgeron and played alongside him in high school and college. "I think that's why he's so emotional. He knows how much it means to the LSU fanbase and Louisiana in general."

A MAN OF THE PEOPLE

LOUISIANA IS HIS HOME. THESE ARE HIS PEOPLE. A hundred miles up the road from Larose, Orgeron moves his refrigerator-sized frame through the front door of a Baton Rouge rib joint, slapping hands with everyone

Ed Orgeron celebrates with his players following LSU's win over Alabama in Tuscaloosa on November 9. (John David Mercer/USA TODAY Sports)

within reach. He passes a "Geaux Tigahs" T-shirt mimicking his Cajun accent and walks to the podium through a whooping and hollering crowd that may as well have been lifted straight from Tiger Stadium.

It's 7 p.m. on a fall Wednesday in Baton Rouge, which means it's time for the Ed Orgeron Show.

The weekly radio show existed under Saban and continued with Miles, who would walk in the back door just before the start of the show. Orgeron has his Tigers poised to potentially replicate the national championship success of the pair of coaches who preceded him, but those men came to the state and left. Louisiana is Orgeron's home. These are his people. And he'll be damned if he walks in the backdoor of TJ Ribs.

"It says he wants these people to touch him, to feel him, to understand he's one of them," said LSU Sports Properties GM Lance Burgos, who has been working the show since the Saban years. "It's a different vibe here now."

It was in this room three years ago that Orgeron held his first radio show as interim head coach after a 2-2 start abruptly ended the Miles era. One fan called and had a conversation in French with the coach. Another LSU diehard, Kent DeJean, greeted Orgeron with a quip as amusing as it was true for south Louisianans: "Finally we have a coach that doesn't have an accent."

"We don't see a lot of Cajun French coaches in the whole country so it's a source of pride," DeJean said in a recent interview. "Sometimes people have negative connotations about Cajuns and think they're not so smart or not hard workers, different ethnic negatives. But by him being successful, he's broken the glass ceiling now and now people take him seriously."

That was not the case when LSU announced the permanent hire of Orgeron, a longtime defensive line coach with only three years of full-time head coaching experience at Ole Miss and a disappointing 10-25 record to show for it.

But Orgeron knew when he accepted his dream job coaching the home team that one game mattered above all.

At the time of his hire, LSU had lost six in a row to Saban's Alabama squad. Homecoming king or not, Orgeron would be nothing unless he took Bama's crown.

"You are judged by that game," Orgeron said at the 2016 press conference. "That's the nature of the beast. And I welcome it. I bring it on. And I can't wait until the day we beat those guys."

AN ELEPHANT OFF THEIR BACK

"THIS IS OUR HOUSE NOW!"

That day came on Nov. 9, when an electrifying 46-41 Game of the Century victory finally knocked the elephant off LSU's back.

Orgeron's emotions burst forth as he took LSU's eight-game losing streak against Alabama and snapped it like a dry branch. Tears turned to battle cries as he huddled his team to officially annex the turf they'd conquered.

"We've been waiting for this moment!" Orgeron roared. "This is our house now!"

It was a legacy-defining win for a man who grew up watching Bear Bryant's Crimson Tide reel off 11 straight against the Tigers. So deeply is the rivalry rooted, Orgeron's father wouldn't even consider Bryant's request to recruit Orgeron to Tuscaloosa out of high school.

So when video leaked of Orgeron's Cuss Heard 'Round the Country, there's a reason the coach didn't apologize for screaming the f-bomb like any lifelong, born-and-bred LSU fan would have done in the Bryant-Denny Stadium locker room. Roll Tide, what?

"I think all people liked it because they see the fire in him," said LSU fan Scott DeJean, Kent's twin brother. "The only people that don't like it are Alabama fans, and it's because they lost."

Back in Louisiana, it was impossible to avoid the good times rolling through Tiger Nation.

Hundreds of fans met the team on the tarmac of the Baton Rouge airport, Gov. John Bel Edwards among them. Orgeron was greeted at his house that night by a yard filled with adoring signs and 30 neighborhood children celebrating his arrival in the driveway.

Ed Orgeron — a Louisiana native — was named LSU's head coach on a permanent basis in November 2016. (John David Mercer/USA TODAY Sports)

"It reminded me of being a kid watching LSU play and what it means to the state," Orgeron said. "It was great to see the joy on those kids' faces."

The next day, at St. Patrick Catholic Church in Baton Rouge, Father Michael Alello began Mass with a homily about six blind men who, together, tried to figure out what an elephant looks like.

Laughter trickled from the pews when he mentioned the elephant.

"I'm not sure how you celebrate Mass without referencing the biggest game of the year," Alello later said.

Is this collective jubilation what Orgeron means by one team, one heartbeat?

"They know I've been through the same things they've gone through," Orgeron said when asked about the outpouring of support. "I represent them. I tell them that all the time. I know how much LSU means to the state of Louisiana, and I know how much the people of the state mean to LSU. I think it's the best place in the world to coach."

The Tigers' victory in Tuscaloosa and subsequent three-win streak to end the regular season has cemented LSU as a contender and Orgeron as a one of the most talked about characters in college football.

In an age of cryptic coaches offering non-answers, Orgeron's willingness to say his team won't celebrate a win over Arkansas "because they haven't beaten anybody in a long time" is refreshing to many. Each Cajun colloquialism dropped during a post-game press conference honors a south Louisiana culture that didn't have a space on the national stage.

And of course, he'll end it with "Go Tigahs."

"You can tell when he's happy. You can tell when he's discouraged. He's very authentic," said LSU fan Charles Kirchem. "I hear that Cajun accent and I just smile. It makes me feel like home."

If anybody in the state can accurately describe the reach of Orgeron's cult of personality, it's Edwards, who admits that LSU's current record — and a campaign fundraiser appearance by Coach O — likely helped his re-election as governor.

"The one thing that sticks out is the state is an easier place to govern when the LSU Tigers and Saints are winning," Edwards said. "During the campaign I've traveled more frequently than normal to every part of our state, and this has unified our state in ways I haven't seen before. Even if they didn't go to LSU, they're still rooting for the Tigers."

A former high school quarterback from Amite who grew up tuning in to Tigers' games on the family radio, the Democratic governor said the outpouring of Tiger pride has everything to do with the school's 33rd head coach and only the third from Louisiana.

"I've been an LSU fan my whole life, and I don't know if we've ever had the level of excitement that we have right now," Edwards said. "And to have that success under a Louisiana head coach who's a native, I think it makes it that much more exciting."

FROM THE BAYOU TO BATON ROUGE

DECADES AGO IN LAFOURCHE PARISH, FOOTBALL WAS A WAY OUT.

Nowhere is that pride felt — or needed — more than the bayous where Orgeron grew up. Life near the predominantly Catholic Mississippi River Delta is planned around a trinity of food, football and faith. But the latter is in short supply as a decline in offshore jobs has fueled an economic downturn.

Kevin Gros, a high school teammate of Orgeron's, said seeing the success of one of their own is a welcome salve in a town where a drop in the price of oil has taken bank accounts with it.

"I got a lump in my throat, because if it wouldn't be for (LSU), I don't know what we'd do," Gros said. "You gotta take the bad with the good and the good with the bad and hopefully the team can win. It's the only thing we got to look forward to, to be honest."

In this part of the state, football season is like hurricane season: a reason to empty the fridge, an excuse to throw a party and a time to hope you don't lose anything. But decades ago in Lafourche Parish, football was a way out.

The son of Ed Orgeron Sr. — known as Baba — and Cornelia "Coco" Orgeron, Bébé grew up playing football in the field across the street from his house, where the sidelines were hedges and a ditch marked half-field. Baba worked for the electrical company and Coco is the daughter of French fur trappers. Both wanted their Bébé to go to college.

Orgeron's brother Steve became a welder, but Coco Orgeron said her first boy was always more of an engine than a mechanic.

"I always said that if that man walked into an auditorium, his presence, you'd know he was going to be the speaker," Coco Orgeron said. "I don't know why, but you'd say, 'That's him.' And he'd shake hands with everybody in the room, including the cook."

After 15 years of fried shrimp, gumbo and chicken fricassee, Larose watched as Bébé grew into a 6-foot-2-inch, 220-pound terror bulldozing into opposing backfields as an All-State defensive lineman for South Lafourche High School.

Larose is and always will be home, where Orgeron returns, as he did as a college freshman after leaving LSU and the coveted scholarship he received.

Hebert says Orgeron didn't take kindly to LSU using him on offense instead of defense. Others say he got homesick. Whatever the reason, Orgeron returned to Larose before the season started and his father gave him a different kind of trench work digging ditches for telephone wires.

"But every time he'd pass (Tiger Stadium), he'd look at it," Coco Orgeron said. "I think he always had that, 'Why didn't I stay?'"

Orgeron's journey back to LSU was a circuitous one.

After he was given a second chance to play college ball at Northwestern State alongside Hebert, Orgeron began to build a reputation for bar fights and late night hijinks. Now 58, Orgeron admitted he did, indeed, put the Ronald McDonald statue in the bleachers.

"We definitely burned the candles at both ends and did things we'd have to run extra for," Hebert said. "And the stories didn't stop after I left."

Gros' favorite Bébé story is when a Northwestern State coach asked Orgeron to deliver a motivational speech to the players as a senior graduate assistant. He told them about two men fishing on a cold day in the same river, with the same pole, the same worms and the same hooks. But only one of them caught fish. After the other fisherman asks what he's doing differently, Coach O explains the successful fisherman's response, Gros said.

"He said, 'You reach in that bucket and put that worm straight on that hook. Not me.' And Coach O pulls a freaking worm straight from his mouth and says, 'I warm mine up before I put him on the hook,'" Gros said laughing. "He had that worm in his mouth the whole time!

"He's a motivator. He'll bring out the best in anybody," Gross said. "You'd never give up around Coach O."

And Orgeron never gave up on his dream of coaching.

His first big break came at the University of Miami, where he emerged as a recruiting maven and coached a defensive line that included future first-round picks Warren Sapp and Cortez Kennedy and a young Dwayne "The Rock" Johnson.

The university also was the beginning of an impressive coaching tree Orgeron would pluck from over the next two decades: Jimmy Johnson and Dennis Erickson led the Hurricanes to two national championships while Orgeron was there. He'd later learn from Paul Pasqualoni at Syracuse, Pete Carroll at USC, Sean Payton on the New Orleans Saints and Monte Kiffin at Tennessee.

"He's an excellent teacher on the field because he's just a guy that pushes people. And he loves the game. Nobody loves the game more than Ed," said former Auburn head coach Tommy Tuberville, then a Miami assistant who roomed with Orgeron for years.

But Orgeron's career path also included setbacks.

He was dismissed from Miami after he headbutted a Baton Rouge bar manager in 1992, a year after a woman accused him of repeatedly attacking her. Orgeron later called the dismissal a necessary step and told media he got sober after marrying his wife Kelly Orgeron.

In 2005, Ole Miss gave Orgeron his first head coaching opportunity after he won two national championships and a Recruiter of the Year award on Carroll's USC staff. But the same fire that made him excel as a defensive line coach caused him to flame out after three seasons at Ole Miss.

Media outlets reported a hard-charging approach highlighted by him challenging his players to wrestle and walking the halls of the athletic facility banging a bass drum.

Orgeron had wanted to infuse the program with the kind of energy he'd grown up with. The morning of high school games, his mother would kick down his door with a shrimp po'boy in one hand and a pompom in the other. On the sidelines at Northwestern State, she was known to climb on the shoulders of cheerleaders.

But that culture didn't quite fit.

Orgeron was fired and again returned to Larose. His mother was neither upset about leaving Rebels fans behind nor about having her son back.

"Every time one looked at me, they asked if I knew how to cook a gumbo. Our 2-year-olds can cook a gumbo! You can't make a conversation with me?" Coco Orgeron said incredulously. "They treated us like we had no mind."

Orgeron would go on to other coaching jobs, but he never lost sight of his ultimate ambition.

David Cheramie, a hometown friend, recalls running into Bébé in 2009 as he was considering a job offer from Tennessee. Cheramie asked what he would do.

"He looked me in the eye and told me that night he was going to be LSU's head coach one day," Cheramie said. "I told him that I had no doubt."

PURPLE AND GOLD PRIDE

WHERE HE'S ALWAYS WANTED TO BE

Orgeron almost wasn't offered the LSU head coaching job.

Despite guiding the Tigers to a 6-2 finish after Miles' dismissal and the season ending with a locker room of players chanting "Keep Coach O!," the hiring of Orgeron was viewed skeptically by many who thought LSU needed the offense of Tom Herman, then the University of Houston's wunderkind head coach.

Three years later, success on the gridiron has transformed Orgeron from a feel-good hire to something closer to a folk hero.

And where other coaching candidates may have come and gone, there's no such fear with Orgeron. He's where he's always wanted to be.

"There's nothing like the feeling of walking the Tiger Walk," Orgeron told a crowd in Larose two months after he was hired. "There's nothing like walking into Tiger Stadium and looking at those guys getting dressed in that purple and gold color and knowing we represent every one of you. Every one of you."

Coach O has gone from a snake-bitten Ole Miss head coach with a 10-25 record to 43-11 since, including eight games as USC's interim. And his eight wins as LSU head coach against Top 25 opponents is already the most in school history.

Now Orgeron's team sits positioned for a run at another championship. And this may be the sweetest of all.

"I think it'd be more special. Les Miles was a carpetbagger coming to Louisiana and even Coach Saban," Hebert said. "They won national championships, and LSU fans can appreciate it. But if they can win this one coming up, it'll be even more appreciated."

THE ED ORGERON SHOW MUST GO ON

"BEING FROM LOUISIANA AND COACHING, IT'S JUST A LITTLE DIFFERENT."

A week and a half after the Tigers' win over Alabama and four days after beating Ole Miss, Orgeron walks in the front door of TJ Ribs, crosses the dining room, gives out the last high-five, and sits down at the purple and gold podium.

He doesn't yet know his team will finish the season 12-0 with a demonstrative 50-7 victory over Texas A&M. Or that his Ohio-born quarterback Joe Burrow will ask to walk onto the field on his senior night with a uniform that reads "Burreaux." Or that he'll walk to the stadium pumping his fist as speakers blare "Born on the Bayou," the song he listened to on his way to accept the LSU head coaching job.

Some call his show to ask questions. Others offer critiques. But most are just dialing in to thank the man who is now, ironically, up for the Bear Bryant Coach of the Year Award.

"Did you ever imagine, after Coach Bear Bryant called your daddy to ask you to play for Bama, you're going to be selected as one of the coaches of the year?"

Ed Orgeron and the LSU players celebrate following LSU's 23-20 win over No. 9 Auburn on October 26. (Derick E. Hingle/USA TODAY Sports)

asked Mike from Alexandria. "That's phenomenal."

As usual, Orgeron deflects the attention.

"Thanks for all the kind words you said, but it's about our football team, and it's always going to be about our football team," Orgeron answers with a slight smile.

Eventually the show ends. Orgeron gives out the last hug and takes the last photo. Only one group is left waiting.

"Hey Bébé! I love you! I love you!"

Orgeron smiles as his honorary aunt and uncle, Paula and Jimmy Guidry, take his hands and clasp them in theirs. Smiling, Orgeron turns and sees another friend he grew up with, Don "Noochie" Adams, and asks the rest of the group what they had to do to drag him to the state capital.

Here, surrounded by his people, Orgeron allows himself to relax. No matter how far he goes from Larose, home has always had a way of finding him.

"There's a lot of pride in the state and a lot of pride for where we come from for what he's doing," Adams said. "Being from Louisiana and coaching, it's just a little different." ■

LSU 66, VANDERBILT 38

SEPTEMBER 21, 2019 • NASHVILLE, TENNESSEE

'BROADWAY JOE' DANCES TO VICTORY

Burrow sets school passing TD record in SEC opener

By Glenn Guilbeau

The Joe Burrow Show reached Broadway on Saturday — the one with honky-tonks and the very stately Vanderbilt University here.

And Broadway Joe," if you will, rocked the block as the front man, tossing the No. 5 Tigers (4-0) to a record smashing, 66-38 victory over the Commodores (0-3, 0-2 Southeastern Conference) in front of 32,048 at Vanderbilt Stadium in LSU's SEC opener.

Roughly, 25,000 of those in attendance were LSU fans, who saw Burrow set the school record with six touchdown passes before the fourth quarter after throwing for the most yards in a half in LSU history with 357 in the first two quarters as the Tigers took a 38-17 lead.

"If we'd have left him in for the fourth quarter, he would have put a hundred on them," LSU coach Ed Orgeron said. "We didn't let that happen. We thought that maybe in the third quarter we would get a drive and then take Joe out, but they kept on scoring. And it was just a little too tight. Joe's a fantastic player. I think there's more to come."

LSU's 66 points was its most in a regulation game since a 70-14 win over Arkansas State in 1991. It was also the third most points allowed in Vanderbilt history and the most since a 66-3 loss to Alabama in 1979.

Burrow, who finished 25-of-34 passing for 398 yards in just over three quarters, also became the first LSU quarterback to throw for 350 yards or more in three consecutive games.

His 16-yard touchdown pass to wide receiver Ja'Marr Chase in the third period set the school TD mark for a game at six — just one short of the season total of TD passes in 2010 for quarterback Jordan Jefferson, who started all 13 games.

"They told me when it happened," Burrow said. "I was more focused on going get another one."

Burrow was gyrating and pointing throughout the first half — throwing it in the face of the Vanderbilt defenders a bit. Vanderbilt defensive end Dayo Odeyingbo and Burrow got into it a bit as the first half ended.

"I told him he was a great player, he played really hard, and I was honored to go against him," Burrow deadpanned sarcastically.

Chase enjoyed seeing his quarterback get feisty.

"Joe is really incredible," Chase, a sophomore,

Joe Burrow set a school record with six touchdown passes in LSU's 66-38 win over Vanderbilt. (Christopher Hanewinckel/USA TODAY Sports)

LSU
LSU

said. "He has his moments. He has that quiet, friendly demeanor about him, but he gets feisty, too. He's real competitive and gets on you or anyone. I like the feisty Joe."

Chase set an LSU record of his own Saturday with four touchdown catches — the most by an LSU receiver in a Southeastern Conference game in history. He caught 10 passes overall for 229 yards, which was the fourth highest total in school history.

"He was all right today, wasn't he?" Burrow said. "Yeah, that's one of the better performances I've seen. Nobody could cover him at all, all day. He was getting open on just about every play. So I was happy for him to have that kind of game."

In four games, Burrow has also already surpassed his total touchdown passes in the 2018 season by one with 17.

"This is who we are," Burrow said. "The first half felt as good as any first half I've had. We're starting to see that we can do this every game against every team."

On the season, Burrow is 100 of 124 for 1,520 yards and 17 TDs with two interceptions.

"He makes plays with his feet. He's very smart," Orgeron said. "I think that Joe is a tremendous football player, especially when he's under pressure."

Backup quarterback Myles Brennan finally replaced Burrow early in the fourth quarter.

"That was one of the better performances I've seen," Burrow said of Chase's day. "He was getting open on just about every play." ■

Racey McMath comes down inbounds for a reception against Vanderbilt. McMath had five catches for 48 yards and one touchdown against the Commodores. (Christopher Hanewinckel/ USA TODAY Sports)

COMMODORES
16
LSU

24 CORNERBACK DEREK STINGLEY JR.

Freshman barely knew grandpa, but thinks of him 'every time I go on the field'

By Glenn Guilbeau • January 1, 2020

Rhe only film clip LSU's Derek Stingley Jr. has seen of his grandfather was "just the hit," as he calls it.

Stingley's grandfather is the late Darryl Stingley, a wide receiver for the New England Patriots who was paralyzed for the rest of his life at age 26 after a hit by Oakland Raiders' safety Jack Tatum in a preseason game in Oakland on Aug. 12, 1978. Stingley, a first-round pick of New England in 1973 out of Purdue, lived as a quadriplegic until he was 55 and died on April 5, 2007, in his native Chicago.

"I've never seen anything else," Stingley Jr. said. "He was going up for a ball. He saw the hit coming, and he just tried to like tense for it. And it just happened. He couldn't really avoid it."

Stingley Jr. was 5 years old when his grandfather died.

"I don't remember that much," he said. "We would go up there for Christmas. And he would always give me a Darth Vader mask and cape and the voice thing. That's pretty much all I remember. And my dad said that he saw something in me back then, but I don't remember."

Derek Stingley Sr., now a defensive back coach at the Dunham School in Baton Rouge and a former Arena Football League player, confirmed that his dad predicted great things for Derek Jr.

"My dad saw him as a young kid," Stingley said. "He ran routes for him when he was 4 or 5 years old. Dad said, 'That boy's going to be special.'"

He was right. Stingley committed to LSU in 2018 as the No. 1 overall prospect in the country out of Dunham. Just a freshman, Stingley Jr. is a consensus first team All-American cornerback in his freshman season at LSU by USA TODAY, The Associated Press, The Sporting News, ESPN and CBS, among others.

"He could be a first-round pick in the next draft," said LSU coach Ed Orgeron, who is glad he will have him for two more seasons. "He is one of the best cornerbacks I have seen."

Stingley Jr. naturally wants to play in the NFL, where his grandfather did for five seasons. The 19th overall selection in 1973, Stingley was coming off his best season in the NFL when he was injured. He had caught 39 passes for 657 yards and five touchdowns with the Patriots in 1977.

"Derek's always been a Patriots fan," Stingley Sr. said. "He gets the history. I think about my dad every day."

Stingley Jr. thinks about him every game.

"I'm just continuing on the Stingley name," he said. "And every time I go on the field, I always think about him. And I think about my dad, and all of my family."

Stingley Sr., a football and baseball star at Orr Academy High in Chicago in the late 1980s, went to Purdue in 1989 like his father before transferring to Triton College in Illinois. He was also drafted, but by

As a true freshman, cornerback Derek Stingley Jr. was a consensus first team All-American. (Derick E. Hingle/USA TODAY Sports)

LSU
24
29
NIKE

Philadelphia of Major League Baseball in the 26th round in 1993. He played professional baseball and later professional football, but did not make it to the NFL or MLB.

"I want to make it to the NFL, but not really because my dad didn't," Stingley Jr. said. "That's just the path I hope I can go. But if not, it is what it is."

Stingley Sr. is trying his best to complete the NFL circle that his dad started. He has been his son's personal coach since he was a toddler, focusing on various hand and football drills ever since Stingley Jr. can remember.

"In my opinion, he's the best coach I've had," he said. "I've had him every year until this year, so he has to be doing something right."

Orgeron would agree, and he has since Stingley Jr. arrived at LSU ready-made.

"I never had a player ready to play like Derek Stingley Jr.," Orgeron said. "And I think his father had a lot to do with it. In fact, I know he did. I'm very good friends with his father. I have a lot of respect for his father. He's an excellent coach, an excellent dad. He and Derek have a really unique relationship."

Not all sons are so receptive of constant coaching by their dad after they reach a certain age.

"Sometimes a coach's son doesn't want his daddy to coach him," Orgeron said. "I remember when I went home, I tried to coach my boys, and they said, 'Dad, I've got a coach.' It just so happens that Coach Stingley is a defensive backfield coach."

And it is working.

"I've come in on Sundays and Saturdays to the indoor facility in the off-season," Orgeron said. "And there was Derek working out with his dad, and he had all the other defensive backs there. Derek Jr. has just a phenomenal work ethic, phenomenal character."

Stingley Jr. says he tries to represent his grandfather and father every time he steps on the field.

"I just think about how I look out there," he said. "And I always want to be the best I can be."

And Stingley Jr. does not think about an injury like the one his grandfather suffered.

"No, that's never really been the talk or anything," he said. "Going on the field thinking about that and playing scared, that's not the way to play." ■

Derek Stingley Jr. steps in front of Georgia receiver George Pickens to intercept a pass during the SEC Championship game. Stingley had two interceptions in LSU's 37-10 win. (Dale Zanine/USA TODAY Sports)

LSU 42, UTAH STATE 6

OCTOBER 5, 2019 • BATON ROUGE, LOUISIANA

'WINNING IS FUN'

Tigers toy with Aggies for 'complete' win

By Glenn Guilbeau

That concludes the passing preliminaries, and what a fireworks show it continues to be.

No. 6 LSU finished its non-conference schedule with an impressive, "complete" 42-6 victory over Utah State in front of about 50,000 by the second half of a game that kicked off at 11 a.m. Saturday in Tiger Stadium.

The fans may not have been all there, literally and figuratively, at kickoff, but Joe Burrow sure was, as he became the first quarterback in LSU history to throw for 300 yards or more in four consecutive games. It was the earliest kick-off at LSU since a 10 a.m., Hurricane Gustav-induced start to the Tigers' 41-13 win over Appalachian State to open the 2008 season.

Burrow finished 27-of-38 passing for 344 yards and five touchdowns before leaving the game after throwing an 8-yard touchdown to tight end Thaddeus Moss for a 42-6 lead with 13:23 still to play.

The win sets up another ESPN GameDay live broadcast at LSU next Saturday to preview the top 10 match-up between the Tigers (5-0, 1-0 Southeaastern Conference) and No. 8 Florida (6-0, 3-0 SEC on ESPN. It will be the first GameDay at LSU since the No. 4 Tigers hosted No. 1 Alabama last year and lost 29-0.

It will be LSU's second GameDay appearance this season as the show was at Texas on Sept. 7 when the No. 6 Tigers beat he No. 10 Longhorns, 45-38.

LSU will be coming off its best overall effort in the win over Utah State.

"It was our most complete game," LSU coach Ed Orgeron said.

Yes, the offense totaled 601 yards in all as tailback Clyde Edwards-Helaire gained 72 yards on 14 carries. And the defense finally showed up by holding a high-flying Utah State offense to just 159 total yards after coming in averaging 533, and to a mere two field goals after coming in averaging 38.5 points a game.

Utah State quarterback Jordan Love came in No. 14 in the nation in passing with 301 yards a game and managed just 130 on 15-of-30 passing with interceptions to safeties Grant Delpit and Kary Vincent Jr. and cornerback Derek Stingley Jr. around two sacks.

Burrow went over 300 yards passing at 315 with 2:54 left in the third quarter on a 39-yard touchdown to wide receiver Justin Jefferson for a 35-6 lead.

The real fun starts next week, and Orgeron was asked if the more pass-happy offense displayed before Utah State would return.

"Winning is fun," he said. "It all depends what the game plan is. I haven't looked at Florida yet. We're going to see what we need to do — maybe go fast, maybe go slow."

Or both. ■

LSU Tigers running back John Emery Jr. ran for 45 yards on eight carries against the Utah State Aggies. (Derick E. Hingle/USA TODAY Sports)

LSU
4

LSU
LSU
9
150
SEC
GRADUATE
Riddell

LSU 42, FLORIDA 28

OCTOBER 12, 2019 • BATON ROUGE, LOUISIANA

BY AIR OR BY LAND

LSU's terrific passing is the talk of a nation, but the Tigers buried Florida

By Glenn Guilbeau

Amid all the breathless excitement, gaudy numbers, and national attention paid to LSU's passing game with Heisman Trophy-contending quarterback Joe Burrow and assistant of the year-challenging pass coordinator Joe Brady, LSU has somewhat quietly become a dangerously balanced offense.

The No. 6 Tigers showcased options Saturday night that eventually twisted and turned No. 7 Florida into submission and into 42-28 losers after the Gators led 28-21 early in the third quarter.

The Tigers' head coaches and offensive coordinators have long lip serviced balance, but never came close.

The 2019 LSU offense is right on it, and it makes the Tigers that much more dangerous, as Florida found out. This team continues to be closer to true balance than perhaps any LSU team in history. The last LSU offense to be less than triple digits away from the same number of passes as runs was the 2001 Tigers, who ran 451 times and passed 411 times.

These Tigers entered the Florida game having passed 188 times and rushed 184 times. LSU showcased its running game for the first time last week in a 42-6 win over Utah State as it rushed for a season-high 248 yards.

"We've just got to see," LSU coach Ed Orgeron said before the Florida game of what his offense may do. "It all depends what the game plan is. But we're going to see what we need to do. Maybe go fast, maybe go slow. Whatever it is, we're going to get it done."

Joe Burrow's passing game earned two thumbs up against No. 7 Florida. LSU's quarterback completed 21 of 24 passes for 293 yards and three touchdowns in the win. (Chuck Cook/USA TODAY Sports)

LSU
9

Or maybe both, which is exactly what LSU did to the Gators and what it will be able to do for the rest of the season against whoever. That includes, you, Alabama.

Against Florida, Burrow threw 24 times, completing 21 for 293 yards and three touchdowns. And LSU rushed 24 times for 221 yards and three touchdowns with junior tailback Clyde Edwards-Helaire gaining 134 on 13 carries for a 10.3-yard average. Through six games, LSU has passed 212 times and rushed 208 times.

LSU never actually went slow, but that may be next on the agenda. Even when it rushed the ball, the drives were fast. A 57-yard run by Edwards-Helaire set up the first touchdown on a 66-yard drive that took two plays and 32 seconds. LSU's third touchdown drive may have taken longer than 1:29, but Edwards-Helaire took care of the last 39 yards by himself for the score.

The Tigers' drive for a 35-28 lead in the third quarter may have lasted longer than 1:41, but freshman tailback Tyrion Davis-Price handled the last 33 on his own for the touchdown.

The Tigers' most time-consuming drive of the night was 3:42 over eight plays and 75 yards, and the longest play was a 19-yard run by Burrow.

LSU could likely be a great running team if it wanted to be, but it will settle for No. 68 in the nation at 165.5 yards a game because it has a nice 4.7-yard per carry average. And LSU would rather be a great overall offense, and it is No. 2 in the nation in total offense at 561 yards a game.

The Tigers gashed Florida over and over with a surgical running game that sliced five runs of 13 yards or more and expertly set up the pass.

In the end against one of the best defenses in the nation, LSU could run against Florida because it could pass, and it could pass because it could run.

When the Gators were thinking pass, offensive coordinator Steve Ensminger would call a run or Burrow would check off to one. When they were bunched in for the run, Brady or Ensminger would call a pass or Burrow would check off to one.

"Great job by Steve Ensminger. I thought he called a tremendous game tonight. Very proud of him," Orgeron said.

It was Ensminger, not Brady or Burrow, who called the dagger to the Gators.

With LSU leading 35-28 with just under six minutes to play, the Tigers had a first down on their 46-yard line. Running play, right? Wrong. Not this LSU team. Ensminger called a sideline bomb to wide receiver Ja'Marr Chase.

"We wanted to put the game away right there," Burrow said.

Chase caught it right in front of the Florida bench in the clear and sprinted the last 35 to 40 yards for the touchdown. The Gators were expecting a run.

"I think the biggest thing is how well we rushed the football," Burrow said. "That was unbelievable. I didn't expect that."

Neither did Florida.

"I think they do a lot better job of running the ball than they get credit for," Florida coach Dan Mullen said. "think people just get really nervous about their passing game, and all the match-ups there. Their backs are good. They find seams and holes."

Edwards-Helaire said now the Tigers are displaying everything they are.

"You can't make us that one-dimensional team and say, 'All they can do is run the ball or just pass the ball,'" Edwards-Helaire said. The former was said about LSU since 2008. The latter has been said since September.

The Tigers can basically take their pick on offense because everything's a click.

"This new offense is shocking, still," said wide receiver Justin Jefferson, who caught 10 passes for

LSU quarterback Joe Burrow celebrates with head coach Ed Orgeron during the fourth quarter. Burrow's 54-yard touchdown pass to Ja'Marr Chase with 5:43 remaining in the game gave the Tigers a 42-28 lead. (Derick E. Hingle/USA TODAY Sports)

123 yards and a touchdown and is No. 7 in the nation with 111.7 yards per game. Chase is No. 6 with 115.6 yards a game after catching seven for 127 and two touchdowns Saturday.

"This offense is tremendous. Coach Brady has done a great job putting in this new offense. We are going to keep throwing the ball, but we can run, too," Jefferson said.

"The progression has been unreal to see," Burrow said of Jefferson and Chase. "Nobody could really stop them all night. I'm really excited about where we are going. We have a chance to be really special. We are going to play our offense. It fits into a lot of different situations run and pass. We have so much more to accomplish. I really feel like we can get there." ■

Above: Defensive end Glen Logan celebrates during the second half. (Chuck Cook/USA TODAY Sports) Opposite: Safety Grant Delpit breaks up a pass in the second half. After the Gators led 28-21 early in the third quarter, the LSU defense held Florida scoreless the rest of the way. (Derick E. Hingle/USA TODAY Sports)

DELPIT
7
SWAIN
VINCENT JR.
5

LSU
150
SEC GRADUATE
LSU
9

LSU 36, MISSISSIPPI STATE 13

OCTOBER 19, 2019 • LSTARKVILLE, MISSISSIPPI

'JOEY BUTTCHEEKS'

Joe Burrow's four touchdowns nearly eclipsed by full moon

By Glenn Guilbeau

Joe Burrow continues to pass LSU quarterbacks just about every time he takes the field.

On Saturday, he threw four touchdown passes in a 36-13 win at Mississippi State that kept the No. 3 Tigers (7-0, 3-0 Southeastern Conference) perfect. His fourth TD gave him 29 for the season. The record was held at 28 by former quarterbacks Matt Mauck in 2003 and JaMarcus Russell in 2006.

The next significant record to fall could be that of quarterback Rohan Davey, who holds the season record for most passing yards at 3,347 set in 2001. Burrow threw for 327 Saturday to give him 2,484, so he is just 863 away.

On Saturday, Burrow even tried to one up the great Y.A. Tittle, LSU's star quarterback from 1945-47. Tittle was a second team All-SEC player in 1946 and '47 before going on to be one of the NFL's greatest in the 1950s and '60s with San Francisco and later in his career with the New York Giants.

Burrow, who has skyrocketed into a top 10 or 14 first-round pick in the NFL Draft over the last two months, could well follow in his footsteps.

Tittle is also known for one of the most infamous plays in college football history on Nov. 1, 1947, when No. 17 LSU was hosting Ole Miss at Tiger Stadium. While playing defensive back in addition to quarterback, which was common at the time, Tittle intercepted a pass from Ole Miss quarterback Charlie Conerly, who would also later become an NFL great with the Giants.

Tittle was in the clear after the pick. He broke a tackle, but that would-be tackler managed to bust Tittle's belt buckle. And his pants went down to about

Joe Burrow's four touchdown passes against Mississippi State gave him 29 on the season, a new LSU record. (Matt Bush/USA TODAY Sports)

his knees before he was eventually tackled. Had he kept his pants, his return could have been longer and maybe LSU would have scored. Instead, Ole Miss won 20-18 and won its first SEC title. The Tigers finished 5-3-1.

It's all in the book "Strange But True Football Stories." You could look it up.

"I never felt so alone in all my life," Tittle said later as he tried to hold the ball with one hand and his pants with the other.

Burrow found himself in a similar predicament Saturday, but with the game well in hand, so to speak, early in the fourth quarter with the Tigers up 36-7. As State defensive end Chauncey Rivers tried to wrestle Burrow to the ground in the pocket, Rivers grabbed at Burrow's trousers and pulled them down.

For a few seconds, Burrow's entire bottom was showcased on CBS national television.

"No comment," Burrow said at first when asked about the wardrobe malfunction.

When politely prodded, though, he did say, "I can honestly say that has never happened before in my life. And hopefully never again."

Burrow explained the play more.

"I felt it coming out," he said. "I heard there was supposed to be a full moon tonight."

And guess who decided to watch Burrow play in person for the first time in his LSU career? Why his grandparents James and Dot Burrow of Amory, Mississippi — just 54 miles north of Mississippi State, where grandpa went to school and played basketball.

And Joe Burrow decided to wear his birthday suit for the occasion.

"My grandparents were here today," Burrow said with sarcasm. "Awesome." ■

LSU running back Clyde Edwards-Helaire rushed for 53 yards on 11 carries in the win over Mississippi State. (Matt Bush/USA TODAY Sports)

CAN'T TOUCH THIS

LSU is a statistical monster

By Glenn Guilbeau • January 5, 2020

The LSU football season has been attached to calculators since game two at Texas, when quarterback Joe Burrow threw for 471 yards in a 45-38 win on Sept. 7 for the second most in history.

Soon Burrow would break the Southeastern Conference record for passing yards and touchdowns in a season, as he has 5,208 and 55 respectively, shattering the previous marks of 4,275 and 44. The yardage record had stood since 1998. Burrow has 71 touchdown passes in his two-year LSU career, which broke the school record of 69 held since 1989 by Tommy Hodson, who played four seasons.

In No. 1 LSU's 63-28 win over No. 4 Oklahoma in a national semifinal in Atlanta, Burrow threw for seven touchdowns and rushed for one, making him the first player in Football Bowl Subdivision history to be responsible for eight touchdowns in a bowl game.

Burrow is the first quarterback in Southeastern Conference history to throw for 5,000 yards and 50 touchdowns in a season. No SEC quarterback had ever thrown for 4,000 yards and 40 touchdowns.

On Dec. 14, he won the first Heisman Trophy for LSU since tailback Billy Cannon in 1959.

The senior from The Plains, Ohio, who transferred from Ohio State in June 2018, is on pace to break the NCAA completion percentage record set by Texas' Colt McCoy in 2008 at .767. Burrow is at .776 (371-of-478 passing) with one game to play. That will be the national championship game between LSU (14-0) and No. 3 Clemson (14-0) on Jan. 13 in the Superdome in New Orleans.

"It's unbelievable what their quarterback has done," said Clemson coach Dabo Swinney, who does have the No. 1 scoring defense in the nation with 11.5 points a game allowed and the No. 1 pass efficiency defense.

"Statistically what he did is unbelievable. They really just shred everybody, and it starts with him," Swinney said.

But it's not just Burrow. Lost in the records and statistics of LSU's magical, stat monster of a 2019 season is the fact that the Tigers are more balanced than one might think. The Tigers have attempted 518 passes on the season, but they have run just 37 fewer times with 481 attempts.

For this reason, LSU has the rare distinction in NCAA history of having a 5,000-yard passer in Burrow, a pair of 1,000-yard wide receivers in Biletnikoff Award winner Ja'Marr Chase (1,559 on 75 catches) and Justin Jefferson (1,434 on 102 catches), and a 1,000-yard rusher in tailback Clyde Edwards-Helaire (1,304 on 199 carries).

They are not the first to achieve such numbers, as previously reported widely, but the Tigers are clearly in rare air.

LSU is the first school since Hawaii in 2010 to have such a voluminous four-pronged attack. Hawaii quarterback Byrant Montz threw for 5,040, while wide receivers Greg Salas and Kealoha Pilares caught passes for 1,889 and 1,306

LSU Tigers wide receiver Ja'Marr Chase poses after scoring on a 50-yard touchdown catch against the Razorbacks. (Stephen Lew/USA TODAY Sports)

LSU
81

yards, and tailback Alex Green rushed for 1,199.

"He's got great receivers, offensive line," Swinney said. "He's had a great run game support. Just a complete football team in every sense of the word."

Many within the LSU locker and meeting rooms anticipated a great passing offense, but not like this.

"No," LSU coach Ed Orgeron said. "I couldn't imagine. I never thought we'd have the records. I thought we could win every game with Joe and the players and the schedule we had with some good teams at home. I didn't know we would. But I had no idea we'd break all the records that we're doing right here."

LSU leads the nation in total offense with 7,899 yards and 564.2 yards a game. The SEC record for total offense was 7,830 set by Alabama last year.in 15 games. Texas A&M had the yards per game record since 2012 with 558.5.

"It's not about the records. It's about the wins," Orgeron said. "But it's been phenomenal — the most prolific offense in SEC history. Nobody ever dreamed that at the beginning of the year."

Burrow's accuracy is unquestioned, and it's not like he throws short very often. But he credits wide receivers Chase and Jefferson in addition to Terrace Marshall Jr. (43 catches, 625 yards), Edwards-Helaire (50 for 399), and tight end Thaddeus Moss (42 for 534).

"We have five NFL guys in route every single snap," Burrow said, excluding running plays to Edwards-Helaire. "So you have to pick your poison. I just try to get the ball in their hands on time and accurately and then let them do the rest."

The passing attack is the brainchild of first-year, 30-year-old pass game coordinator Joe Brady, whom Orgeron hired from a lower offensive assistant job with the New Orleans Saints.

"The last thing I told Joe was he was making a mistake," Saints coach Sean Payton said on Friday. "So much for what I know. But look, I'm excited certainly for Ed and their staff and that team. It's been really impressive."

And it looks very familiar.

"I know when I watch them on TV and that's what I've seen — they just have such good balance," said Payton, who has had some of the NFL's best offenses since 2006. "They're running the ball well. There's a lot of talented players on the field. The quarterback has been outstanding. It is impressive. We are their biggest fans. We're excited for them. It's a good time to be a football fan in Louisiana."

As when Saints quarterback Drew Brees usually drops back, Burrow does not always have an intended receiver. This spreads the wealth.

"Everybody eats. We've been saying that since the spring," Jefferson said.

"It's making them defend every single person," Burrow said. "Anybody can get the ball on any play. We're not designing plays to go to this one guy. We have progression reads that everyone can get the ball on until I decide. So you have to be on your toes as a defense and really understand who has each individual player. Otherwise, we'll beat you, or I'll find a guy. And that's what makes it so difficult to defend."

LSU safety Grant Delpit noticed that in the spring as the defense struggled to focus on a receiver or two as in the past.

"Just seeing Joe slinging the ball around, getting the ball into play makers' hands was great to see. We knew we had a great team then," he said.

"We do a really good job of finding match-ups that are favorable to us," Burrow said. "You've got to find your guy."

But there are too many as the numbers suggest.

"We make it difficult to do that," Burrow said. ■

Quarterback Joe Burrow had a season unlike any other in SEC history, becoming the first quarterback ever in the conference to throw for 5,000 yards and 50 touchdowns in a season. (Jason Getz/USA TODAY Sports)

LSU 23, AUBURN 20

OCTOBER 26, 2019 • BATON ROUGE, LOUISIANA

'SEC GAMES AREN'T GOING TO BE PRETTY'

LSU and Burrow bounce back from adversity and a nasty hit to beat Auburn

By Glenn Guilbeau

Can a Heisman moment happen when you get creamed by a defender?

Wouldn't look good as a statue, understood.

Perhaps such a scenario should be worthy of votes, if you get right back up the way LSU quarterback and Heisman Trophy contender Joe Burrow did following a viciously efficient — and legal — hit by cornerback Javaris Davis during the No. 3 Tigers' 23-20 win over No. 10 Auburn at Tiger Stadium.

At the time, Burrow had thrown for only 42 yards. He had completed 8-of-9, but only for 5.2 yards a completion. And LSU was trailing 3-0 at the time following its first shutout in a first quarter since losing 29-0 to Alabama last season.

The hit by Davis just as Burrow was about to go out of bounds after a 14-yard scramble on third-and-12 from his 9-yard line took the breath out of Tiger Stadium. And it looked like it took more than that out of Burrow — the rugged senior transfer from Ohio State who continues to carry LSU (8-0, 4-0 Southeastern Conference) to glory on his back.

Teammates rushed to the Auburn sideline to see how he was.

And he popped right back up like a kids' Popeye punching bag filled with sand at the bottom.

"That's what I try to do," Burrow said. "Taking hits and getting right back up. If you lay down on the field and don't hop right back up, it shows your team that you're not really into it."

Burrow's into it.

After handing off to tailback Clyde Edwards-Helaire on the next play, these were Burrow's next six plays — all passes:

- 6 yards to tight end Thaddeus Moss.
- 6 yards to wide receiver Ja'Marr Chase.
- incomplete to Justin Jefferson.
- 19 yards to Chase.
- 27 yards to Chase.
- 20-yard touchdown to wide receiver Terrace Marshall Jr.

Burrow finished with another Heisman-like performance — 32-of-42 passing for 321 yards with the

LSU Tigers cornerback Derek Stingley Jr. intercepts a pass intended for Auburn Tigers wide receiver Seth Williams in the second quarter at Tiger Stadium. (Chuck Cook/USA TODAY Sports)

AUBURN
18
24

6

touchdown while rushing 13 times for 31 yards (after 16 yards lost on three sacks) with a 7-yard touchdown on a designed draw play for a comfortable, 23-13 lead with 13:29 to play. Hurried three times by Auburn's rush, he was dodging and darting all day long, and even tip-toed down the sideline with a near Heisman statue stiff arm at one point.

LSU should have scored a lot more as it outgained Auburn 508 to 287, but the offense was just off on this day because Auburn's defense is for real. Burrow's three sacks were all in the first half, though, as the Tigers adjusted. He did throw an interception with LSU down 13-10 in the third quarter. Chase was covered well by Auburn cornerback Roger McCreary at the Auburn goal line, but Burrow threw it anyway for a one-on-one try. It didn't work.

Freshman superstar Derek Stingley Jr. also fumbled a punt return that set up an Auburn field goal to give it a 10-7 lead in the second quarter.

Opposite: Terrence Marshall Jr. had two catches in the win over Auburn, including one for a touchdown. (Chuck Cook/USA TODAY Sports) Above: LSU quarterback Joe Burrow runs past Auburn Tigers defensive back Christian Tutt in the 23-20 LSU win. (Chuck Cook/USA TODAY Sports)

LSU
68
9
LSU

"We showed toughness today," Burrow said. "It was not a pretty win by any means. SEC games aren't going to be pretty. When you can come out on top of a top 10 team and feel like you could have played better, it's always a good thing."

When Auburn still led 13-10 late in the third quarter after LSU blew two red zone scoring chances — one on Burrow's interception and the other after four plays inside the Auburn 3-yard line failed to score — LSU could have stayed down.

"I think a lesser team would not have won that game," LSU coach Ed Orgeron said. "Adversity hit us. We weren't playing very well."

And LSU bounced back up after it found itself trailing in a game later than at any point this season when Auburn led 13-10 until the final minutes of the third quarter. And this after LSU out-gained Auburn 237 to 147 in the first half and 431 to 222 through three.

"It did feel weird," Burrow said. "It did. We had 508 yards of total offense and only scored 23 points. We are going to have to get better in short-yardage situations and the red zone. But it was nice to see us win in a different way."

LSU beat a very good team when it did not play well. That says something. It means Burrow and his boys will figure they can still always win in a variety of ways even if they play poorly at times. That happens in national championship seasons. ■

Joe Burrow runs for a fourth quarter touchdown, giving LSU a 23-13 lead. (Chuck Cook/USA TODAY Sports)

LSU

LSU 46, ALABAMA 41

NOVEMBER 9, 2019 • TUSCALOOSA, ALABAMA

'THIS IS OUR HOUSE FROM NOW ON'

LSU finally beats Bama

By Glenn Guilbeau

The most losses any current LSU football player, such as the few fifth-year seniors on the team, personally has against Alabama is four.

Most of the team has three or less.

But even the true freshmen, who are undefeated against Alabama at 1-0 after No. 1 LSU's 46-41 win over the No. 1 Crimson Tide (No. 1 in the USA TODAY coaches' poll and at No. 3 in the CFP poll) here Saturday night, felt the weight of 0-8.

"Oh, yeah, even the freshmen," said LSU junior linebacker Patrick Queen, who is from Ventress, a town of 1,200 or so 30 minutes north of Baton Rouge.

"When you come to LSU, you know that family bond," said Queen, whose interception of Tua Tagovailoa and 16-yard return with a personal foul against Bama for 13 more to the Tide's 13 with 11 seconds to go in the first half set up a touchdown for a 33-13 lead.

"It ties you in with what this program has been through," Queen said.

LSU had gone through eight straight losses to its bullying big brother:

- 21-0 ... Jan. 9, 2011, for the national championship in LSU's backyard at the Mercedes-Benz Superdome in New Orleans. ... LSU never crossed the 50 until the fourth quarter.
- 21-17 ... Nov. 3, 2012, at home. ... LSU led 17-14 in the final minutes.
- 38-17 ... Nov. 9, 2013, in Tuscaloosa. ... LSU could've taken a 7-0 lead on its first possession, but fullback J.C. Copeland fumbled at the 1.

LSU Tigers quarterback Joe Burrow and head coach Ed Orgeron hug in celebration after defeating the Alabama Crimson Tide 46-41. (Butch Dill/USA TODAY Sports)

- 20-13 in overtime ... Nov. 8, 2014, at home. ... LSU could've taken a 17-10 lead in the final minute after recovering a fumble at the Alabama 6. But LSU guard Vadal Alexander was whistled for a 15-yard unsportsmanlike conduct penalty. LSU settled for a field goal, and Bama came back.
- 30-16 ... Nov. 7, 2015, in Tuscaloosa. ... LSU came in at No. 2 in the nation, and tailback Leonard Fournette was running away with the Heisman. And then nothing.
- 10-0 ... Nov. 5, 2016, at home. ... Alabama was holding on quarterback Jalen Hurts' touchdown, but if it is called, LSU still loses, 3-0.
- 24-10 ... Nov. 4, 2017, in Tuscaloosa. ... LSU played well. And after the game, an enthused Coach Ed Orgeron said, 'We coming. We coming. And we ain't backing down."
- 29-0 ... Nov. 3, 2018, at home ... LSU didn't go anywhere.

But now, it's over.

"Being able to snap that streak, that was a big blessing for us," Queen said.

LSU quarterback Joe Burrow was only 0-1 against Alabama, but he knew all about the weight lifted off the Tigers' shoulders as he rode off the field victorious on the shoulders of defensive linemen Tyler Shelvin and Jakori Savage.

"That was pretty special, having these guys embrace me the way they have," Burrow said after throwing for 393 yards and three touchdowns and rushing for another 64. "Some quarterback from Ohio that came in last June before the season, and the way they have embraced me, I can't say. I mean it means a lot to me that this entire program has embraced me and the whole state as well."

Burrow did just beat Alabama, and he put LSU (9-0, 5-0 Southeastern Conference) in position to reach the College Football Playoffs for the first time and win a national championship for the first time since the 2007 season.

"This is why I decided to transfer," Burrow said. "I wanted to play, and I knew I could play on this stage. And I got great people around me, great coaching staff, great program all-around. And I cannot say enough good things about my offensive line tonight."

Burrow was sacked five times, but he was able to hit several of his 31 completions in 39 attempts just as he was about to be hit or was being hit.

"We're going to be as good as we want to be. We can get there," Burrow said.

Orgeron was 0-3 with two shutout losses against Alabama in his first three seasons as head coach and 0-4, counting his 2015 season as an assistant at LSU. Orgeron, 58, also grew up in LaRose, a town of 7,000 on the bayou, and thus lived the 0-11 record LSU had against Alabama from 1971-81.

"It's been a long time coming," he said. "We felt it all week, that we were the better football team. I said to our team on Monday, 'We're the better football team, but we have to play to prove it.'"

Orgeron was still feeling it as LSU touched down here Friday before its six touchdowns and 46 points — the most either team has scored in the history of the series that dates back to 1895.

"You know, when I got on the plane coming here, I felt like, 'We've got it. We've finally got the tools we need. We've finally got the players we need. We've finally got the coaching staff we need to beat these guys,'" Orgeron told himself.

He said that to offensive coordinator Steve Ensminger, who was 0-for-4 as a quarterback at LSU against Bama from 1976-79 and 0-for-the-last-8 as an assistant coach.

"I felt it was a combination of going to a spread on offense and obviously the great recruiting,"

Orgeron said. "Those great receivers, and Joe Burrow. To have a championship team, you have to have a championship quarterback."

Wide receiver Ja'Marr Chase caught six of Burrow's passes for 140 yards. Wide receiver Justin Jefferson caught seven for 79 yards and the desperate Alabama onside kick at the end of the game to seal it.

Tailback Clyde Edwards-Helaire grabbed nine passes for 77 yards, including a 13-yard touchdown for the 33-13 lead with :06 remaining before half after the Queen interception. The 20-point LSU bulge was its largest lead over Alabama since a 27-3 win in 2003 when Nick Saban coached the Tigers to the national championship.

Edwards-Helaire rushed for 103 yards on 20 carries and three touchdowns, which was the most rushing touchdowns by a back against Alabama under Saban, who took over in 2007.

"So, I felt like we had it," Orgeron said. "I knew we had to do it, and we did it."

LSU players went wild on the field after the game as if they had won a national championship.

"LSU players are celebrating like they haven't beat Alabama in eight years," the Voice of Alabama Football Eli Gold said as the game ended. "And they are very deserving."

LSU has arrived in the Alabama series again, and then some. The Tide surrendered its most points ever under Saban, who had not allowed more than 46 as a head coach since he was at Michigan State in a 51-28 loss at Penn State in 1998.

New LSU pass game coordinator Joe Brady, meanwhile, went to 1-0 all-time against Alabama and left a mark on Saban — the defensive genius.

"We couldn't stop them," Saban said. "They have no weaknesses on offense. It's nothing like what they tried to do a year ago."

Saban's and Alabama's 31-game home winning streak fell along with their 8-0 run against LSU home and away. The Tide's last home loss was on Sept. 19, 2015 — 43-37 to Ole Miss.

Orgeron, who famously said, "We coming. We coming, and we ain't backing down," after a 24-10 loss by the Tigers the last time he was here in 2017, was asked if they were there yet.

"Yeah. We were there tonight for sure," Orgeron said.

First Alabama, now the world?

"We'll see where this leads us," Orgeron said. "We took a big step in beating Alabama obviously. I knew we were the better team. I didn't think we were out-physical-ed at all. I thought we handled them physically. They made some plays. We made some plays. I think we are right there where we need to be."

Queen feels that, too.

"We're going to be a team to look out for," he said.

And probably not just for this season.

"This is our house from now on," Orgeron screamed to his team in a postgame huddle. Before the game, he had told his players, "Eight is enough." And he wasn't talking about a 1970s television show.

"They beat us for eight years. We got tired of hearing their stuff, man," Orgeron said on ESPN after the game. "I mean it was time. I told the team, 'We draw the line. We had enough. Here we come.'" ■

THE NIGHT THE TIDE DIED

16 moments to never forget from LSU's victory over Bama

By Glenn Guilbeau • November 15, 2019

After one of the greatest opening guitar riffs in rock history, Lynyrd Skynrd lead singer Ronnie Van Zant says, "Turn it up" moments before kickoff at University of Alabama home football games, and the crowd goes wild in Bryant-Denny Stadium.

Then Van Zant sings the "Sweet Home Alabama" opening line:

Big wheels keep on turning.

But on Nov. 9, 2019, LSU stopped the wheel, sticking a dagger in the spokes of an eight-game winning streak by the Crimson Tide over the Tigers that started with a 21-0 win on Jan. 9, 2012, for the national championship, and ran over LSU seasons that could have been national championship bound in 2012, 2015, and 2018.

Not this time. LSU never trailed, led by 20 at the half, and held on for a 46-41 win over Alabama in front of 101,821 at a place LSU basically turned into its own Denny's.

Here are 16 moments to never forget from "The Night the Tide Died ... for LSU."

1. RASHARD LAWRENCE BATS IT AWAY: Alabama quarterback Tua Tagovailoa showed no signs of tightrope ankle surgery just three weeks prior as he completed a 20-yard pass to wide receiver Henry Ruggs III on the first play of the game before tailback Najee Harris gained 31 around right end. Then on second-and-goal from the LSU 8-yard line, Tagovailoa rolled left and had Harris open inside the 5. But defensive end Rashard Lawrence knocked it down. With a completion there for a touchdown or for a short-yardage third down, the next play may never have happened as it did.

2. PHANTOM FUMBLE: On third-and-goal at the LSU 8-yard line, Tagovailoa rolled right and suddenly could not decide to run or throw. Maybe with a good ankle, he could have tried to push his way by safety Grant Delpit for the touchdown. Then, untouched, he just dropped the ball.

Let's credit the forced fumble to former LSU coach Les Miles. Who knows?

Linebacker Ray Thornton, who was playing for suspended starting linebacker Michael Divinity Jr., recovered at the 8-yard line. Alabama coach Nick Saban was caught shaking his head in disgust on the sidelines for the first of many times. And Alabama never the same, as it never snapped the ball again with a chance to take the lead.

It wasn't all luck, though. LSU's defensive game plan was not to contain Tagovailoa in the pocket — rather force him out for scrambles on his bad ankle. As the game wore on, he could not run as well as he could when the game opened.

3. CLYDE EDWARDS-HELAIRE DOES IT ALL: The LSU tailback rushed for 103 yards on 20 carries, caught a career-high nine passes for 77 with his first career touchdown reception of 13 yards for the 33-13 halftime lead, and returned a kickoff 19 yards in which he was not actually brought to the ground.

But Edwards-Helaire also set a pick for Alabama

Tigers quarterback Joe Burrow celebrates as teammates hoist him after their historic win over Alabama. (Butch Dill/USA TODAY Sports)

LSU
9
BRENNAN
15
89
ANDIE

cornerback Patrick Surtain II, who was an LSU commitment until the 11th hour before signing day in 2018, enabling wide receiver Ja'Marr Chase to get open. Quarterback Joe Burrow hit Chase for 23 yards to the LSU 49-yard line and was 1-for-1 on the day. Two plays later, Burrow found Chase for a 33-yard touchdown and 7-0 lead with 9:15 to play in the first quarter. LSU led the rest of the way. And Burrow — 3-for-3 for 74 yards — and his Heisman train was on their way to a 31-of-39 passing game for 393 yards and three touchdowns.

4. PHANTOM SNAP: Alabama deep snapper Thomas Fletcher snapped it perfectly to punter Ty Perine on fourth-and-6 from the LSU 41, but Perine just dropped it, like Tua. He recovered but lost 19 yards. LSU took over on Alabama's 40. Burrow threw an interception on first down, though, to cornerback Trevon Diggs at the 20. But defensive end Raekwon Davis was whistled for being the 12th man on the field, and the interception was nullified by, yes, Saban sideline mismanagement. Like Perine, Davis wears No. 99. It was only halfway through the first quarter, and Alabama already had made three critical mistakes. Moments later, Cade York kicked a 40-yard field for a 10-0 LSU lead with 4:54 to go in the first quarter.

5. WADDLE SHOULD HAVE FALLEN DOWN: The Tigers let Alabama get back in the game at 10-7 on a 77-yard punt return for a touchdown by Jaylen Waddle with 1:14 left in the first quarter. LSU's Racey McMath had a clear shot at him just as he caught the punt, but McMath went in too high and grabbed Waddle's face mask. Then he let it go, trying not to get the penalty. He should have just continued on with the face mask tackle as he had already committed it. It would have been a 15-yard penalty — not a touchdown. It was the first touchdown on a punt return allowed by LSU since Javier Arenas ran one back 61 yards to give the Tide a 34-27 lead with 7:33 to go in the fourth quarter in 2007 at Bryant-Denny. The Tigers won that one, too, 41-34.

6. "EMBARRASSING" ALABAMA DEFENSE: Many LSU fans love to complain about the television commentary of their Tigers, but there was nothing to whine about in this one. When LSU took a 16-7 lead on a 29-yard touchdown pass from Burrow to wide receiver Terrace Marshall Jr. with 13:03 to go in the second quarter, both play-by-play announcer Brad Nessler and color man Gary Danielson let Alabama have it.

And they should have. Three LSU receivers were open on the play — Marshall and tight end Thaddeus Moss in the middle of the secondary and Edwards-Helaire in an empty right flat. Moss could have also scored a touchdown on the play, and Edwards-Helaire likely would have had a long gain.

"Marshall had time to put up his left hand and say, 'Joe, I'm right here. Throw it to me,'" Nessler said.

"Holy Cow! You see busts on one once in a while, but two like that! Embarrassing for the Alabama defense," Danielson said, missing the open Edwards-Helaire.

"The first word that comes to mind for Alabama is mistakes," Danielson continued.

"And sloppy," Nessler said.

7. SWEET AND QUIET ALABAMA: With LSU in command at 16-7 and with more points than in its three previous games against Alabama combined (10), Bryant-Denny fell into shock and awe as CBS panned the audience.

"Saw that shot of the crowd. Everybody's stunned in here," a salty Nessler said. "The biggest eruption was the applause for the president and the playing of 'Sweet Home Alabama.' Only thing to cheer about is the punt return so far."

8. CADE YORK DELIVERS: One of the biggest concerns from LSU fans and Coach Ed Orgeron going into the Alabama game was freshman LSU kicker Cade York. He delivered with a second field goal — a 45-yard booth for a 19-13 lead with 4:20 to play in the first half.

9. THADDEUS MOSS' TWO-STEP: LSU tight end Thaddeus Moss is not a Cajun, but he performed the best two-step Orgeron, who is clearly Cajun, may have ever seen for a spectacular catch. Moss was out of bounds as a pass from Burrow was in flight to him, and he got back in just in time and just in bounds for a 16-yard catch at the Alabama 1-yard line.

Tigers wide receiver Terrace Marshall Jr. (6) celebrates his touchdown with tight end Thaddeus Moss (81) during the second quarter of the huge win over Bama. (John David Mercer/USA TODAY Sports)

TIGERS
MARSHALL JR.
6
81
LSU

"That's Randy-esque," Danielson said in reference to Hall of Fame NFL wide receiver Randy Moss, who is Thaddeus' father.

The play was reviewed, and it was determined that cornerback Trevon Diggs pushed Moss out, so it was legal for Moss to re-establish himself in bounds. But this call was made in Tuscaloosa — 57 miles from the SEC office in Birmingham that LSU fans incorrectly feel is biased toward Alabama.

"About time," Orgeron smiled at his press conference Monday. "Hey, when we got that call, I said, 'It's our day.' And I want to say, that was the best officiated game that I've ever been a part of. I thought those guys did a tremendous job officiating the game, and I called Steve and told him that. When we got that catch, when that catch was not overturned, I wasn't complaining about anything else, man."

Three plays later, Edwards-Helaire scored on a 1-yard run for a 26-13 LSU lead with 26 seconds to go before halftime.

10. GONE IN 20 SECONDS: Tagovailoa's second turnover of the half clinched the game for LSU, though there were some nervous moments in the second half as Alabama kept coming back. But it never tied LSU or took the lead, thanks to two touchdowns by LSU over the final 26 seconds of the first half. After LSU went up 26-13, linebacker Patrick Queen intercepted Tua and returned it 13 yards to the Alabama 26-yard line with 11 seconds to go in the half.

The Tigers got 13 more yards (half the distance to the goal) for an unnecessary roughness call against center Landon Dickerson after the interception. Dickerson nailed LSU safety Kary Vincent Jr. after the play from behind.

"That's about as cheap a shot as I've seen in a while," Danielson said.

On the next play, Burrow hit Edwards-Helaire for a 13-yard touchdown and 33-13 lead with six seconds left in the half.

"I don't believe I'm saying this — LSU by 20," Nessler said and got saltier still. "Alabama's behind the 8 ball and all the other balls in the rack."

11. THE WAVE: Burrow performed the opposite of the mocking, delicate Queen's wave he displayed late in the win at Texas this season when he and other Tigers did the "Bring It" wave — four fingers toward yourself — as they ran into the locker room at the half. Other LSU players ran off with their hands to their ears as if to say to the Bama fans, "Can't hear you."

12. COULD'VE BEEN EASIER: LSU could have put the game away much earlier than it did as it received the third quarter kickoff with a 20-point lead and promptly drove to the Alabama 36-yard line the old-fashioned way. Edwards-Helaire gained 6, 7, and 18 along the way. LSU was looking at a 36-13 lead at worse, or 40-13. And that could've been 40-6 if McMath finishes tackling Waddle's face mask on the punt return.

Instead, Burrow fumbled it to Terrell Lewis after a sack by Xavier McKinney. And Alabama got back in the game and shook up the LSU Nation. Alabama also converted three fourth downs on its two back-to-back touchdown drives to get within 39-34 in the fourth quarter.

13. THE CLYDE DRIVE: When LSU took over on its 25-yard line with 14:33 to play in the game, Alabama had the momentum, a suddenly aroused home crowd, and it had LSU worried after back-to-back touchdowns drives cut LSU's lead to 33-27.

On second-and-3, Edwards-Helaire gained 12 over left guard, shedding and bulling over tacklers in his wake. The next play was just a 6-yard completion from Burrow to Chase, but it exemplified once more why Edwards-Helaire is still LSU's starting tailback, and one of the highly recruited freshmen is not yet.

Safety Shyheim Carter blitzed Burrow on first down and had a clear path, but Edwards-Helaire went low on him and tripped him as Burrow had enough time for the completion.

Four plays later, LSU faced a critical third-and-10 from Alabama's 36-yard line. Alabama edge rusher Anfernee Jennings got to Burrow, but as Burrow was falling down, he got it to Edwards-Helaire, who had to reach way down to get it. It looked like he would come up five or six yards short of the first down, but he just ran over and through Diggs and safety Jared Mayden to just get the first down.

"We had a chance to stop them on third-and-10 once,"

Saban grimaced. "Got to give (Edwards-Helaire) a lot of credit. He ran through a guy for four or five more yards to get a first down."

Edwards-Helaire kept churning for a 6-yard gain, then scored the touchdown for LSU's 39-27 lead with 10:07 to go on a 5-yard run after breaking a tackle by McKinney behind the line and spinning left.

Alabama will not soon forget No. 22.

14. KEVIN FAULK'S FACE: After LSU went up 39-27, CBS showed Burrow on the bench on the phone to the pressbox. In front of Burrow was former LSU tailback and present director of player development Kevin Faulk. He couldn't have been smiling wider as he twirled a victory towel while jumping up and down. Faulk was 1-3 against Alabama as a player.

15. HELL'S BELLS FOR BAMA, NOT LSU: LSU rewrote another song during this game. Alabama plays the foreboding opening of AC/DC's "Hells Bells" when an opponent faces a third down. LSU is familiar with the tune. It was 3-of-11 on third down when it totaled 182 yards in a 30-16 loss in Tuscaloosa in 2015 as the No. 2 team in the nation.

On this day, LSU was 8-of-15 on third down, including 4-for-4 to end the game. There were three third-down conversions on "Clyde's Drive" for the 39-27 lead in the fourth quarter — a 13-yard catch over the middle by wide receiver Justin Jefferson on third-and-3, Edwards-Helaire's 11-yard catch on third-and-10, and a 15-yard quarterback draw by Burrow to the 5-yard line that caught Alabama completely off guard.

After Alabama cut it to 39-34 with 5:32 to play, Burrow pulled the quarterback draw again on third-and-2 from the Alabama 25 for 18 yards as Saban just threw up his hands. Burrow could've thrown up a Heisman pose on that run as he finished with 64 rushing yards on 14 carries and 457 overall. Edwards-Helaire scored on a 7-yard run on the next play for a 46-34 lead with 1:37 left.

It wasn't a third down conversion, but LSU needed one more first down to finally put Alabama to bed after the Tide drew within 46-41 with 1:21 left on an 85-yard Tagovailoa bomb to Devonta Smith against Derek Stingley Jr. with LSU inexplicably not in a prevent defense. And Edwards-Helaire bulled over more would-be Bama tacklers for 12 yards on first down, and it was over.

16. SWEET HOME LOUISIANA: "This is amazing," Edwards-Helaire said on CBS after the game. "Can't wait to get back home."

Little did he and the rest of the Tigers know what was waiting for them at Baton Rouge Metropolitan Airport — hundreds of LSU fans meeting the team like they were the Beatles.

"Louisiana, I love you," Burrow, the Athens, Ohio, native tweeted upon his last touchdown — the one in Baton Rouge.

"I didn't really realize how much this meant to Louisiana," Burrow said Monday of the airport greeting. "It was pretty special. I was very surprised to see it, and I wanted to do anything I could to embrace those people who came out. That was awesome. I was excited to see all those people. I'm starting to realize how much that game meant to people. It's just been an onslaught from a bunch of people. Everyone had their eyes on that game."

Yes, 16.6 million people watched the LSU-Bama game, which was not even a prime-time game. It was the most watched college football game on any network, CBS reported, since No. 1 LSU beat No. 2 Alabama, 9-6, in overtime on Nov. 5, 2011 — the last time LSU beat Alabama. That game in prime time drew 20.11 million.

When Orgeron returned home, there were signs in his front yard. This usually happens when a coach is about to get fired. But these said, "We love you, Coach O."

Then he and his wife Kelly did what many LSU fans did Saturday night — watched the highlights on ESPN.

"Went home Saturday night, me and Kelly, had a ham sandwich and some chips, and watched SportsCenter," Orgeron said. "I mean, it was a great night." ■

LSU 58, OLE MISS 37

NOVEMBER 16, 2019 • OXFORD, MISSISSIPPI

NO BAMA HANGOVER, BUT NO DEFENSE EITHER

Tigers roll Ole Miss in scoring fest

By Glenn Guilbeau

No. 1 LSU put its emotional win over Alabama last week in its rear-view mirror Saturday night and held off Ole Miss for a 58-37 victory at Vaught-Hemingway Stadium behind another record-smashing performance by quarterback Joe Burrow.

Burrow broke the LSU record for most passing yards in a season held by Rohan Davey since 2001 in the second quarter when he went over Davey's 3,347-yard mark and later finished with 3,687.

Burrow also broke the school mark for consecutive completions with 17 — 16 to end the first half and one to start the third quarter. Four quarterbacks held the previous LSU record of 14 consecutive completions — Chad Loup against Arkansas in 1993, Matt Mauck against Louisiana Tech in 2003, and JaMarcus Russell against Mississippi State in 2006.

The senior from Athens, Ohio, finished the game with 32 completions in 42 attempts for a career-high 489 yards and five touchdowns with two interceptions. The 489 yards is second in school history only to Davey's 528 in a 35-21 win at Alabama in 2001.

Ja'Marr Chase broke the school record for receiving touchdowns in a season with his 13th in the win, as he caught eight passes in all for 227 yards and three touchdowns that were all long plays — 34, 51, and 61 yards. All eight of his catches were for first downs and touchdowns.

"I'm a physical receiver," Chase said. "I like to put my head down, get the first down, fight for extra yards. That's the type of receiver I am. It's part of my game. It's something that I have to try to do. It's something that I just do."

The Tigers totaled a whopping 714 yards, which was second in school history to the 746 gained against

Tigers wide receiver Justin Jefferson runs with the ball during the second quarter of the dominant offensive performance against Ole Miss. (Vasha Hunt-USA TODAY Sports)

LSU
36
LSU
36
38
38

Rice in a 77-0 victory in 1977. But LSU allowed 614 yards to a 4-7 team.

"We gained 700 yards, but everyone's upset in the locker room," Burrow said.

The Tigers allowed 30 points and 405 yards in the second half alone as it let the Rebels back in the game after leading 31-7 at the half.

Ole Miss freshman quarterback John Rhys Plumlee set the school record for rushing yards by a quarterback with 212 on 21 carries with four touchdowns.

"We won it by 21 points, but obviously when you don't play well on defense at LSU, nobody's feeling good," LSU coach Ed Orgeron said. "That's just the way it is." ■

Opposite: Tigers kicker Cade York kicks against the Rebels with punter Zach Von Rosenberg holding. (Vasha Hunt/USA TODAY Sports). Above: Running back Tyrion Davis-Price salutes the fans after he ran in for a touchdown during the first quarter of the big win. (Vasha Hunt/USA TODAY Sports)

LSU 56, ARKANSAS 20

NOVEMBER 23, 2019 • BATON ROUGE, LOUISIANA

HOW THE SEC WEST WAS WON

LSU roasts Arkansas to secure spot in SEC Championship Game

By Glenn Guilbeau

No. 1 LSU won its first Southeastern Conference West title since 2011 with a 56-20 roasting of Arkansas on Saturday night at Tiger Stadium and will play No. 4 Georgia for the SEC championship on Dec. 7 in Atlanta.

"We're 11-0. We're proud of that, but we're not done yet," LSU coach Ed Orgeron said. "There'll be no celebrating tonight. It's a goal of ours, but we've got bigger goals."

The Tigers (11-0, 7-0 SEC) will next meet No. 24 Texas A&M (7-4, 4-3 SEC) on Nov. 30 to end the regular season in Tiger Stadium. Even with a loss to the Aggies and a win by Alabama at Auburn on Nov. 30, LSU would still win the West at 7-1 by head-to-head tiebreaker over a 7-1 Alabama, which lost to LSU. Georgia (10-1, 7-1 SEC) beat Texas A&M, 19-13, on Saturday.

LSU last won the overall SEC title also in 2011 at 13-0 overall and 8-0 in the SEC before losing the national championship game to Alabama.

"There'll be time to celebrate what we've done," Orgeron said.

Tailback Clyde Edwards-Helaire led LSU with a career-high 188 yards on only six rushes with touchdown runs of 89, 27, and 26 yards. He averaged 31.3 yards a carry, which would break the LSU record for average yards per rush held by Harvey Williams at 19.6 set against Rice in 1987. But that record requires a minimum of 10 rushes.

Edwards-Helaire also caught seven passes for 65 yards.

"He's on fire," Orgeron said of Edwards-Helaire. "Unbelievable. His vision, the spin, the cut. Outstanding. Great back."

LSU quarterback Joe Burrow completed 23 of 28 passes for 327 yards and three touchdowns before leaving the game late in the third quarter.

The Tigers led 28-6 at halftime and finished off Arkansas (2-9, 0-7 SEC) quickly on their second possession of the third quarter.

In 43 seconds, LSU covered 85 yards in two plays and made SEC history.

First, Edwards-Helaire ripped a 35-yard run to midfield. From there, Burrow found a wide open Ja'Marr Chase down the middle of the field for a 50-yard touchdown and 35-6 lead with 7:48 to go in the third quarter.

The run put Edwards-Helaire over 1,000 yards for the season at 1,031, and the pass put Burrow over 4,000

Tigers wide receiver Ja'Marr Chase reacts after scoring a 50-yard touchdown in LSU's 56-20 win against Arkansas. (Stephen Lew/USA TODAY Sports)

150
SEC
LSU
1

LSU
17
LSU

yards passing at 4,014 at the time. With Chase and wide receiver Justin Jefferson already each over 1,000 yards receiving entering the game, LSU became the first school in SEC history to have a 4,000-yard quarterback, two 1,000-yard receivers, and a 1,000-yard rusher.

"I didn't think at the beginning of the year that Clyde would get 1,000 yards," Orgeron said. "He's a competitive cat, man."

The Tigers made it 42-6 less than two minutes later as Edwards-Helaire scored on a 26-yard run. LSU increased that to 49-6 on an 89-yard run by Edwards-Helaire with 2:46 left in the third quarter on his last run of the game.

"It parted like the Red Sea," Edwards-Helaire said. "Everybody talks about breakaway speed. I hope that was fast enough for everybody."

Myles Brennan replaced Burrow before that Edwards-Helaire run.

LSU out-gained Arkansas 612 yards to 304.

Freshman tailback John Emery Jr. replaced Edwards-Helaire early in the fourth quarter and scored on a 39-yard run for a 56-6 lead.

Arkansas cut LSU's lead to 56-13 midway in the fourth quarter on a 24-yard pass from quarterback Jack Lindsey to wide receiver Mike Woods. After LSU's kick return team failed to retrieve an onside kick until it rolled to the LSU 11-yard line, Arkansas tailback Devwah Whaley scored on a 2-yard run to get the Hogs within 56-20 with 6:56 to play.

Arkansas lost its 18th straight SEC game in the debut of interim coach Barry Lunney Jr.

"There's not going to be a big celebration after beating Arkansas," Orgeron said. "They haven't beaten anybody in a long time." ■

Tigers wide receiver Racey McMath carries the ball against the Razorbacks during the first half at Tiger Stadium. (Stephen Lew/ USA TODAY Sports)

'IT PARTED LIKE THE RED SEA'

Clyde Edwards-Helaire goes 89 yards for mic-drop TD

By John Marcase • November 23, 2019

Ed Orgeron had seen enough of Clyde Edwards-Helaire on Saturday night.

With the top-ranked Tigers comfortably ahead of woeful Arkansas in the third quarter, Orgeron was ready to give his junior running back the rest of the night off.

However, Edwards-Helaire needed one yard to reach 100 for the game, so LSU's offensive coaching staff talked Orgeron into giving him one more carry.

It resulted in an 89-yard touchdown run that electrified what was left of the Tiger Stadium crowd of 101,173 and highlighted LSU's 56-20 victory over the Razorbacks.

"I got to tell y'all the truth," confessed Orgeron. "That play, when they went in, I said 'Hey guys, don't you think it's about time to get Clyde out?' They said just one more play, Coach. They felt like they were gonna make a big play, and that was the one play, so I'm glad they didn't take him out until after that play."

Edwards-Helaire knew he had 99 yards rushing when his number was called.

"I was in on that conversation," he said. "I was pretty much done at that moment. They were like you need a yard to get 100 yards. I went in and it was like get the yard, get out of bounds and shut it down for the game.

"Man, it parted like the Red Sea."

Arkansas' Myles Mason nearly caught up to Edwards-Helaire at the Razorback 25, but a timely high-step eluded Mason's attempted tackle.

Earlier in the game, Edwards-Helaire caught a Joe Burrow pass on a crossing route and was tripped up. He made sure that did not happen on the 89-yard run.

"I seen an amazing-size hole and I ran through it," said Edwards-Helaire. "It was me understanding that nine times out of 10, usually it is one guy to beat, especially when a hole opens up like that."

Edwards-Helaire accounted for 253 total yards and 3 touchdowns. He actually caught more passes (7) than he had rushes (6) but those six carries netted 188 yards and three touchdowns. His 31.3 yards per carry against the Razorbacks would've easily set a school record, but it didn't qualify, falling short of the 10 minimum carries. Harvey Williams' 19.6-yard average set against Rice in 1987 is safe, for now.

"He's on fire," said Orgeron. "We really like Clyde, obviously. He is starting to learn how to hit the holes. This spread offense fits him well. He's perfect for it. ... He knows where that hole is and usually the first guy can't tackle him."

In his last four games, Edwards-Helaire has rushed for 599 yards, eclipsing the 100-yard rushing mark in each game for the 11-0 Tigers.

Saturday, he reached 1,000 yards for the season, and now has 1,146 yards on the season. That makes LSU the first team in SEC history with a 4,000-yard passer (Burrow), two 1,000-yard receivers (Ja'Marr Chase and Justin Jefferson), and a 1,000-yard back (Edwards-Helaire).

"I didn't think at the beginning of the season he was going to get 1,000 yards," admitted Orgeron. "Give him credit. He is a competitive cat."

Orgeron may have had his doubts, but not Burrow.

"I knew it from the moment I got here last year Clyde was a special player," said Burrow, the Heisman Trophy front-runner. "I knew that this offense was a perfect fit for him, just like that guy (Alvin Kamara) over there in New Orleans.

"He's great out of the backfield, and when they bring an extra defensive back to cover him, he can run it, too."

Edwards-Helaire said it is just a matter of being ready.

"If your number is called, make the play," he said. "It is the offense. We just get better at it each week." ■

Clyde Edwards-Helaire finishes off an 89-yard touchdown run against Arkansas during the second half at Tiger Stadium. (Stephen Lew/USA TODAY Sports)

150
LSU
22
10

LSU 50, TEXAS A&M 7

NOVEMBER 30, 2019 • BATON ROUGE, LOUISIANA

LSU TO TEXAS A&M: 'YOU COMPLETE ME'

Tigers save best overall game in regular season for last

By Glenn Guilbeau

"YOU COMPLETE ME," Tom Cruise told Texan Renee Zellweger in the movie "Jerry Maguire."

Cruise, who was playing Maguire, was declaring his love for Zellweger's character, Dorothy Boyd, after they had split up in the 1996 classic.

LSU in no way loves Texas A&M. In fact, LSU's players and coaches love to hate the Aggies more than any other opponent lately — more than even Alabama because of A&M's questionable, 74-72, win in seven overtimes last year at this time that was followed by an ugly fight started by A&M assistant and former LSU assistant Dameyune Craig.

"We spent the entire year thinking about those (expletive deleted)," one LSU staff member said while pointing to the A&M bench as the No. 1 Tigers celebrated their 50-7 revenge-soaked victory over A&M Saturday night at Tiger Stadium with a little more class.

Here's a hint. The expletive starts with the same letter that Aggies does.

But more than revenge, which may be best served cold but is at its best short-sighted, No. 1 LSU saved its most "complete" game of the regular season for Texas A&M and for last. And that will serve the Tigers (12-0, 8-0 Southeastern Conference) better down the road in the SEC Championship Game Saturday in Atlanta against No. 4 Georgia (11-1, 7-1 SEC) and beyond — no matter how cold, empty, and thoroughly beaten the Aggies (7-5, 4-4 SEC) were as they left Tiger Stadium.

And this just four days after College Football Playoff committee chairman Rob Mullens basically said Ohio State was a more "complete" team than LSU. And up until Saturday, that was clearly true.

"To date, their defense is not as strong as Ohio State's," Mullens said after his committee flip-flopped No. 1 LSU and No. 2 Ohio State.

That may still be true after Saturday, but LSU's defense took a major step toward LSU's ultimate completion as the Tigers stepped on A&M's collective face.

"You complete me," LSU coach Ed Orgeron could have told Texas A&M coach and former LSU coaching candidate Jimbo Fisher after the game. Fisher's offense managed season lows for total yards and passing offense with 169 and 97 yards, respectively.

"You complete me," LSU outside linebacker K'Lavon Chaisson could have told Texas A&M junior

LSU Tigers nose tackle Siaki Ika signals a safety against the Texas A&M Aggies in the second half of a 50-7 win. (Chuck Cook/USA TODAY Sports)

62

3
LSU
LSU
FARM
BUREAU
INSURANCE
GAME 1

quarterback Kellen Mond, whom he sacked 1.5 times and whom LSU sacked five times in all along with five hurries.

It was Mond who said the following at the SEC Media Days last July about the overtime win: "As you could see a lot of the LSU players were cramping, and obviously we were standing tall on both sides of the ball."

Not now. It was Mond who had one of the worst games of his career here Saturday night — 10 of 30 for 92 yards and three interceptions.

"You complete me," LSU defensive coordinator Dave Aranda, whose defense has often been incomplete this season, could have told Fisher, who tried to hire him away from LSU when he was taking over at A&M after the 2017 season.

"They kicked our butts on all three phases — offense, defense, and special teams," Fisher said. "Kellen was harassed all night."

Yes, LSU was telling Aggie jokes all night long as it outgained A&M, 553 yards to 169 and totaled 31 first downs to 12.

"It was what we have been looking for all year," Orgeron said. "This is overall a tremendous night, an overall package. I am so proud of Coach Aranda. What a difference a year makes."

Yes, on Dec. 1, 2018, LSU was 9-3 and 5-3 and in yet another slow burn about the SEC office following some controversial calls and no-calls in the A&M loss.

On Dec. 1, 2019, LSU is the new Alabama (10-2, 6-2 SEC), which has two regular season losses for the first time since 2010 after falling, 48-45, at Auburn Saturday night.

That kind of "completes" this magical season for LSU, too. Alabama will NOT be in the playoffs for the first time since that format began in 2014, and LSU will be for the first time if it beats Georgia, and maybe even if it does not.

"That was the LSU standard of performance," Orgeron said. "So many great things happened tonight. We are happy to be 12-0. Tremendous job by our staff. But you know what, we ain't done yet."

Much more to come, particularly from quarterback Joe Burrow, who did the usual as he "completed" 22-of-32 passes for 352 yards and three touchdowns. In the process, he set the SEC record for passing yards in a season with 4,366, breaking the mark of 4,275 set by Kentucky's Tim Couch that had stood since 1998 when "Jerry Maguire" was fresh on VHS. Burrow also tied the SEC mark for touchdown passes in a season set by Missouri's Drew Lock with 44 in 2017.

But he wanted to talk about LSU's defense.

"I think the defense wanted to send a message to the country," Burrow said. "They've been criticized the last few weeks, and that's what they've been talking about all week."

LSU's defense was the missing link. A&M's offense is not close to great, but the Tigers' defense at least ended the regular season on an upswing and looking like it could at least play with Ohio State, Clemson, Oklahoma, or whoever.

As long as it has Joe Burrow.

"I've said it all along after watching tape," said Fisher, who lost to Clemson this season. "He is playing as good as anybody. LSU's offense is outstanding."

Yes, Texas A&M completed LSU.

But you had me at Burrow. ■

Tigers safety JaCoby Stevens intercepts a pass against Aggies quarterback Kellen Mond during the second half at Tiger Stadium. (Stephen Lew/USA TODAY Sports)

MISFIT TOYS SOAR FOR LSU

Orgeron, Burrow and other Tigers overcame adversity

By Glenn Guilbeau • December 3, 2019

Nebraska, where Joe Burrow's dad Jimmy was a Sugar Bowl hero defensive back in 1974 and where Joe's two brothers Jamie and Dan played football, didn't want him.

Ole Miss and Mississippi State, which were on opposite sides of where his dad grew up in Amory, Mississippi, and where his uncle Johnny and grandfather James played football and basketball, respectively, didn't want Joe Burrow either.

Alabama coach Nick Saban and other coaches told Catholic High tailback Clyde Edwards-Helaire he was a kick returner ... only.

Junior center Lloyd Cushenberry was the last signee of LSU's 2016 class as a lowly two-star prospect on a scale of five stars out of Dutchtown High in Geismar — 17 miles from LSU's campus. LSU had not been overly interested for two years, and he committed to Mississippi State on Jan. 22. But on Feb. 2, 2016 — the day before signing day — LSU got interested and offered a scholarship.

Junior wide receiver Justin Jefferson was also a two-star signee in LSU's 2017 class out of Destrehan High. His only other offer was from Nicholls State.

Things did not work out for Thaddeus Moss, the No. 6 tight end in the nation in 2016, at North Carolina State, and he transferred to LSU in 2017, sat out that season, and missed 2018 with a foot injury.

Things have not worked out well for LSU coach Ed Orgeron a few times.

An LSU signee in 1979 as a lineman out of South Lafourche High, he just didn't like it and left after a few weeks of practice, went to work on phone lines back home on the bayou, and transferred to Northwestern State the next year.

After five years as an assistant coach with the Miami Hurricanes, he was fired after the 1992 season and didn't coach again until 1994 back home at Nicholls State. He was fired after three seasons as Ole Miss' head coach in 2007. He was interim coach at USC in 2013, but did not get the job. He took 2014 off with his only regular "work" being a weekly guest spot on a Baton Rouge radio show.

And look at them now.

Two of Orgeron's wins this season came over coaches who were considered to be LSU's head coach before he got the job after serving as interim head coach during the 2016 regular season. Those were Texas' Tom Herman (45-38 loss on Sept. 7) and Texas A&M's Jimbo Fisher (50-7 loss on Nov. 30).

"I'm sure he thinks about it," Burrow said of his coach. "Just like I think about beating teams that didn't recruit me or counted me out. But we're ... sitting on top of the world right now."

"I've fought through a lot of adversity," Burrow said after beating Texas A&M as LSU completed just its third regular season ever unbeaten and untied.

"A lot of people on our team have gone through a lot of adversity," Burrow said.

Yes, there was a time when things were not going well

Tigers running back Clyde Edwards-Helaire was told he would only be a kick returner in college by several of the schools that recruited him, including Alabama. (Dale Zanine/USA TODAY Sports)

LSU
20
26

even for Burrow and several other key LSU players who are in the midst of the season of their lives.

Late in preseason practices for the 2017 season, Burrow, a red-shirt sophomore at Ohio State out of Athens High in Athens, Ohio, broke his right throwing hand in a non-contact drill. This after he likely had just taken the lead for the backup job to starter J.T. Barrett in the last scrimmage before the season.

"Me and Dwayne Haskins were battling it out for two years at that point," Burrow said. "And they were getting ready to name a backup. And I broke my hand."

A linebacker rushed Burrow in the non-contact drill, and somehow hit Burrow's hand with his helmet.

"It just got caught up in there," Burrow's father said. "Basically, it was a freak deal. He had played well enough in the scrimmage that we thought he still had the edge. We'll never know."

While Burrow was out with the injury, Haskins had established himself as the backup and would win the job over the next spring.

"I kind of knew it was over at Ohio State then," Burrow said of his thoughts just after the injury. "I didn't know what I was going to do."

Listed as out for four to six weeks, he tried to rehabilitate the hand and came back quicker than expected. But it was frustrating.

"My hand was that fat," Burrow said, widening his left hand over his right hand to the size of a small football. "I couldn't throw. I tried to throw after two weeks, but they were wobbles. Wobbles all over the place because I broke my hand. Didn't know what I was going to do, because I knew my time there was probably over. And I was trying to figure out what I was going to do."

Less than a year later, he had graduated from Ohio State and was at LSU with two years to play. In May 2018, over crawfish at Mike Anderson's on Lee Drive in Baton Rouge, he convinced Orgeron and offensive coordinator Steve Ensminger he could do it at LSU. And they promised Joe and his dad that they would change the offense — eventually.

"They didn't know if it was going to work," Burrow said. "We kind of took a chance on each other. It's worked out perfectly. Coach O sold me on his vision of what's going on this year. And I sold Coach O and the staff on what I could do as well. So, it was kind of a perfect match. And the rest is history."

Meanwhile, Edwards-Helaire, in some circles, was not going to be the starting tailback for LSU in 2019. One LSU staff member on signing day last February said it would be 6-foot-0 true freshman signee John Emery Jr., the No. 2 tailback in the nation out of Destrehan High who had de-committed from Georgia to LSU.

The 5-8 Edwards-Helaire, who is now listed at a gracious 5-9, was a three-star who was the No. 23 tailback in the nation in 2017. He is not only the starter this season. He finished the regular season No. 4 in the SEC in rushing with 102.8 yards a game and 1,233 on the season with a league-high 16 touchdowns.

"Let's see if this small guy can do this for us," Edwards-Helaire said, imitating coaches and teammates over the years. "And then it's like, 'Oh, my God, he's actually good.' It's not like, 'I told you so,' but I'll be like, 'I know what I can do.' The people in my corner knew what I could do. The people who watched me grow up knew."

Orgeron even doubted Edwards-Helaire would be this good.

"I think nobody thought that he'd have the great year that he's had," said Orgeron, who had planned to use Emery and fellow true freshman tailback Tyrion Davis-Price more. "I thought he'd be a good back, no question about that. I didn't think he'd gain 1,000 yards. But he's exceeded all of our expectations, except Clyde's expectations."

Cushenberry is in his second year as LSU's starting center and probably its best offensive lineman. He could go in the middle rounds of the 2020 NFL Draft if he leaves a year early.

Jefferson led LSU in receiving last season with 54 catches for 875 yards and finished the regular season second to Ja'Marr Chase with 81 receptions for 1,092 yards and 13 touchdowns. He is No. 15 in the nation with 6.8 catches a game.

Moss, a senior, set the LSU record this season for most catches by a tight end as he has 36 for 423 yards. Malcolm Scott had held the record at 34 since 1981.

"Lloyd was the last guy signed in the '16 class," Burrow said. "Thad was a transfer. Justin was a two-star guy. Clyde was always too short. We have so many guys who have fought through adversity. Coach O — fired two places. And I think

Tigers wide receiver Justin Jefferson was a two-star recruit out of high school, only receiving scholarship offers from LSU and Nicholls State. (Derick E. Hingle/USA TODAY Sports)

that's really helped us become who we are."

Orgeron did not mention his own story and his firings to motivate his players. He didn't have to.

"I think they know it. I think a lot of you have written about it a lot," he said at his press conference Monday with a wry smile. "I think it's very well-documented. I think the guys read that. We don't talk about that. But you know what, (Burrow) mentioned that. He mentioned that to someone. I think it brings up a good point. That it doesn't matter."

When Saints coach Sean Payton hired Orgeron to his first and last NFL job following the 2007 season to be an assistant after Ole Miss had fired him, Payton said something that has stuck with Orgeron.

"I remember being with Sean Payton," Orgeron said. "It was my first NFL meeting. I was a little nervous. I didn't know what to expect, coaching NFL players."

And Payton said, "It doesn't matter how you got here. You're here. Now, make the best of it."

Burrow, Edwards-Helaire, Cushenberry, Jefferson, Moss, and Orgeron have done just that.

"That's what these players are doing," Orgeron said. "And that's what I do." ■

MARSHALL JR.
6
14
7

SEC CHAMPIONSHIP GAME

LSU 37, GEORGIA 10

DECEMBER 7, 2019 • ATLANTA, GEORGIA

SEC CHAMPIONS

Defense dominates Dawgs

By Glenn Guilbeau

Quarterback Joe Burrow has made No. 1 LSU's offense the talk of the nation as he soars toward the Heisman Trophy and the College Football Playoff semifinal against No. 4 Oklahoma on Dec. 28 in Atlanta.

But Burrow has also helped LSU's defense on the side. No, he's not playing safety, though he probably could.

"Joe taught me a lot," LSU freshman cornerback Derek Stingley Jr. said after intercepting two passes in the Tigers' 37-10 win over No. 4 Georgia in the Southeastern Conference Championship Game Saturday in Mercedes-Benz Stadium.

"In high school, I was always able to make the play, but when I came here, and Joe had pinpoint accuracy, there were just times that I was on the receiver, but I just couldn't do anything about it," Stingley said. "That just taught me a lot about the game because it's going to happen."

Stingley gave up few completions as he also made five tackles and had a pass breakup Saturday. His first interception of Georgia quarterback Jake Fromm came on a first-down pass with the Bulldogs on LSU's 40-yard line late in the first half with the game still somewhat in doubt with the Tigers up, 17-3.

Stingley caught the pass intended for wide receiver Tyler Simmons at the 13-yard line, and LSU stayed up 17-3 at the half.

"This game proved the point because a lot of people, they didn't really respect us as a defense," Stingley said. "But we came out and played and showed everybody what we're made of."

Georgia Bulldogs defensive back DJ Daniel defends LSU Tigers wide receiver Terrace Marshall Jr. in the second quarter of LSU's SEC Championship Game victory. (Brett Davis/USA TODAY Sports)

27
LSU
LSU
JEFFERSON

Georgia did not get into the end zone until the fourth quarter, and its 286 total yards were its second lowest of the season.

"On defense, it was amazing. This is what we've been working for since the summer," Stingley said. "We knew that if everybody worked together, then nobody could really compete with us."

Stingley became the first player in the SEC title game to intercept two passes since Florida's Lito Sheppard had two in the 2000 game.

"In case anybody forgets, Derek is a freshman. In case anybody forgets that. I forget a lot," Burrow said.

"He's one of the finest corners I've ever been around," LSU coach Ed Orgeron said. "And he's a competitor."

Georgia coach Kirby Smart also acknowledged LSU's dominant play.

"We just couldn't make enough plays tonight," Smart said. "I give LSU a ton of credit. That is a really good football team, and we knew that coming in. We were going to have to play well. We were going to have to make explosive plays. We were unable to do that."

Opposite: Justin Jefferson had a big performance in LSU's win, with seven catches for 115 yards and a touchdown. (Brett Davis/USA TODAY Sports) Above: LSU quarterback Joe Burrow fist bumps head coach Ed Orgeron with his wife Kelly Orgeron as they celebrate their 37-10 victory over Georgia in the 2019 SEC Championship. (John David Mercer/USA TODAY Sports)

40
LSU
1
LSU

Georgia had no play longer than 21 yards.

"That's not what we thought was going to happen," Smart said.

Orgeron did.

"I wasn't surprised," he said. "Preparation. I thought these guys were phenomenal."

The win was LSU's 12th SEC football championship overall — 1935, '36, '58, '61, '70, '86, '88, 2001, '03, '07, '11, and '19.

The Tigers will be in the playoffs for the first time since the current final four format began in the 2014 season. LSU is now two wins away from its first national championship since the 2007 season.

"Tonight wasn't our final destination," Orgeron said. "We know that." ■

Opposite: LSU wide receiver Ja'Marr Chase celebrates a touchdown, one of his three catches in the game. (John David Mercer/USA TODAY Sports) Above: Offensive lineman Austin Deculus does a snow angel in confetti after triumphing in the SEC Championship Game. (Jason Getz/USA TODAY Sports)

LSU
2019 SEC FOOTBALL
CHAMPIONS
TIGERS
8-14
LSU
CHAMPIONS
TIGERS
IT JUST MEANS MORE

LSU Tigers players react on the set of ESPN SEC Network after continuing their perfect season in the SEC Championship Game. (Dale Zanine/USA TODAY Sports)

NISSAN
MAN
HE
THE HEISMAN MEMORIAL TROPHY
PRESENTED BY
THE HEISMAN TROPHY TRUST
TO
JOE BURROW
LSU
AS THE OUTSTANDING COLLEGE FOOTBALL PLAYER
IN THE UNITED STATES FOR
2019

9

QUARTERBACK

JOE BURROW

Heisman Trophy is 'for LSU, Ohio State, southeast Ohio, and all of Louisiana'

By Glenn Guilbeau • December 15, 2019

LSU's first Heisman Trophy won by halfback Billy "Atomic" Cannon happened so long ago — 60 years ago as of Dec. 9, 2019 — it was almost like it didn't really happen.

Viewing olden times, black-and-white, newsreel footage of the event with then-vice president Richard M. Nixon giving Cannon the award in the Downtown Athletic Club in New York City makes you feel as if you're watching a Hollywood movie as opposed to real, reel life.

In fact, the 1988 movie set at LSU and loosely based on the Frank Deford novel of the same name, "Everybody's All-American," plays out somewhat like the fairy-tale, but flawed, ultimately victorious life of Cannon. And it actually opens with strikingly similar newsreel footage of a 1956 star Louisiana halfback named Gavin Grey as played by Dennis Quaid.

They filmed parts of the movie in Tiger Stadium in 1987 during games with fans dressed in suits and hats, which was game night attire at the time. Quaid with the same classic crew cut Cannon wore was standing right there on the sidelines next to reporters as Alabama beat LSU, 22-10. This all just added to the mythology that ran alongside Cannon's story book Halloween Night Run to the Heisman in 1959 for six decades and five days.

LSU won the Sugar Bowl, albeit played in Tiger Stadium, for the national championship in the movie with Grey scoring the winning touchdown against Georgia as time ran out.

The Hollywood-like tale of LSU and the Heisman was updated in color and embellished with truth Saturday night on ESPN at the PlayStation Theater in Manhattan.

Quarterback Joe Burrow, whose family is from Mississippi, as was Cannon's, won the award as college football's greatest player after he led the Tigers to a story book, 46-41 victory at Alabama on Nov. 9 and to the SEC championship last week with a 37-10 win over Georgia. This one is new and true and even more fairy tale like as Burrow was not even seen listed as top 10 Heisman candidate last summer with 200-to-1 odds to win it.

Cannon's college career was storybook with a national championship in 1958, but without a happy ending, as LSU had only one more game to play after he won the '59 Heisman. The Tigers, 9-1 at the time and No. 3 in the nation, lost unceremoniously, 21-0, to No. 2 Ole Miss in the Sugar Bowl on Jan. 1, 1960, in Tulane Stadium in New Orleans at a time when final polls came out before bowls.

Burrow won the award with fantasy-like, "atomic" numbers during the season and in the voting.

He brought in the highest completion percentage in NCAA history at 77.9 on 342-of-439 passing for a SEC record 4,715 yards and a SEC record 48 touchdowns.

He left with the highest vote margin in Heisman history at 1,846 points, beating the previous mark of USC tailback O.J. Simpson, who won in 1968 by 1,750

Joe Burrow was a longshot to win the Heisman Trophy entering the 2019 season, yet ended up winning the prestigious award with the highest vote margin in Heisman history. (Brad Penner/USA Today Sports)

PREMIER PARTNER OF
NISSAN
THE HEISMAN MEMORIAL TROPHY
PRESENTED BY
THE HEISMAN TROPHY TRUST
TO
JOE BURROW
LSU
AS THE OUTSTANDING COLLEGE FOOTBALL PLAYER
IN THE UNITED STATES FOR
2019

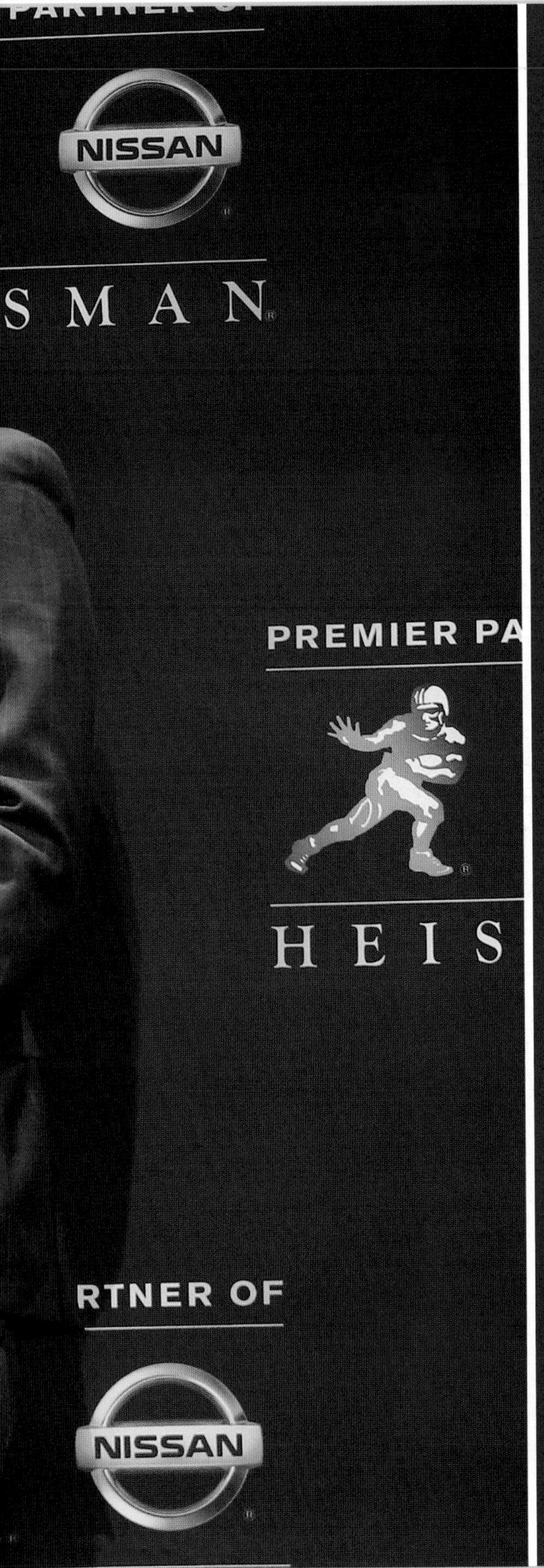

points. His 90.7 percent of the first place votes beat the record of 86.7 percent held by Ohio State quarterback Troy Smith since 2006.

"Love you, so proud of you," his mom, Robin Burrow, said with a kiss on his way to the podium.

"You're the man," his dad, Jimmy Burrow, said as he hugged him.

"Proud of you," LSU coach Ed Orgeron said with another hug.

Burrow went on to greet Louisiana Gov. John Bel Edwards, Louisiana Senate President John Alario, LSU athletic director Scott Woodward, pass game coordinator Joe Brady, offensive coordinator Steve Ensminger and others.

Then Burrow delivered one of the very best acceptance speeches in the 85-year history of the award and its most emotional since Penn State running back John Cappelletti's tearful tribute in 1973 to his dying, 10-year-old brother Joey, who died three years later of leukemia.

"Whew," Burrow said at the podium. "First thing I want to say is," and he had to stop.

Twelve seconds went by as Burrow got choked up and applause broke out. Eight more second went by as he tried to compose himself.

"I want to thank my offensive line first," he said. But he still couldn't go on and knocked on the podium.

Then he giggled and put fingers to his crying eyes before listing those linemen — left tackle Saahdiq Charles, left guards Adrian Magee and Ed Ingram, center Lloyd Cushenberry, right guard Damien Lewis, and right tackles Austin Deculus and Badara Traore. He went on to mention tight end Thaddeus Moss, wide receivers Ja'Marr Chase, Terrace Marshall Jr., and Justin Jefferson.

"All my teammates have supported me, welcomed me with open arms — a kid from Ohio coming down to the bayou and welcoming me as brothers," he said.

"It's an honor to stand on the same stage as all of you guys," Burrow said while turning to the row of previous Heisman recipients with Notre Dame's Paul Hornung (1956), USC's Mike Garrett (1965), and

Heisman Trophy winner Joe Burrow poses with the trophy and head coach Ed Orgeron during a post-ceremony press conference. (Brad Penner/USA Today Sports)

Florida's Steve Spurrier (1966) seated closest to him.

Nebraska receiver/back Johnny Rodgers, who won the award in 1972 and played with Jimmy Burrow at Nebraska, was also close by along with USC tailback Marcus Allen (1981) and Boston College quarterback Doug Flutie (1984).

"It's just an honor to be on the same stage and eat dinner with you guys. It's been so awesome, and you've all been so kind to me," he said. "My parents. My dad — first time in 51 years that he wasn't a player or coach. Him retiring this year (to watch all his son's games in person) has been a dream come true for me and my family. My brothers in the audience (former Nebraska players Jamie and Dan).

"I'm just so thankful for LSU and Ohio State (where Burrow was at from 2015 through the spring of 2018 before transferring to LSU). Playing at two of the best programs in the country, great coaches at both places. My journey, I wouldn't have traded it for anything in the world."

Burrow acknowledged the other Heisman finalists seated — Hurts, Ohio State defensive end Chase Young in third and Ohio State quarterback Justin Fields in fourth. Like Burrow, Hurts and Fields are transfers.

"I tried to leave a legacy of hard work and dedication and preparation and loyalty wherever I go," Burrow said. "I'm surrounded by such great people that make that so easy."

Then Burrow, a native of The Plains, Ohio, in Athens County, took his speech to a unique place — reaching out to those less fortunate.

"Coming from southeast Ohio, it's a very impoverished area," he said. "There are so many people that don't have a lot. And I'm up here for all those kids in Athens and Athens County that go home to not a lot of food on the table, hungry after school. And you guys can be up here, too."

After another round of applause, Burrow addressed the residents of another state with some of the most impoverished areas as well.

"I'd like to thank Louisiana, the entire state," he said to more applause. "Like I said earlier — just a kid from Ohio coming down, chasing a dream. And the entire state has welcomed me and my family with open arms and invited us to be native Louisianians. I've learned to love crawfish and gumbo."

Also a true story.

"He's a full Louisiana guy now," LSU defensive end and Monroe native Rashard Lawrence said after Burrow donned a jersey with "Burreaux" on the back for Senior Night against Texas A&M on Nov. 30. "Oh yeah, man, he's always in the cafeteria eating gumbo and turkey legs and everything. I don't know if we've got him sucking the heads on crawfish yet, but we're working on it."

Burrow knows what follows football season here.

"During crawfish season, Coach O makes sure we have pounds and pounds and pounds of crawfish," Burrow said. Then he teared up again, started tapping the podium.

"Take your time," someone from the audience shouted as Burrow gathered himself once more.

"You have no idea what you mean to my family," he said to Orgeron with his voice shaking and his nose sniffling. "You know, I didn't play for three years. You took a chance on me, not knowing if I could play or not."

Burrow paused and took a weary, teary breath.

"I'm forever in your," he whimpered and stopped again. "I'm forever grateful for you. Can you imagine a guy like Coach O giving me the keys to his football program? He just means so much to me and my family and to LSU. I sure hope they give him a lifetime contract because he deserves it."

Robin and Jimmy Burrow laughed, and Robin kissed the hand of Orgeron's wife Kelly.

"So, thank you to everyone," Burrow said. "So when I lift this trophy again, it's for LSU, Ohio State, southeast Ohio, and all of Louisiana. Thank you."

Roll credits.

The End.

For now. ■

Joe Burrow tears up during his emotional and memorable Heisman Trophy acceptance speech. (Todd Van Emst/Heisman Trust/Pool Photo/ USA TODAY Sports)

81
SOONERS
10

PEACH BOWL

LSU 63, OKLAHOMA 28
DECEMBER 28, 2019 • ATLANTA, GEORGIA

LSU LANDSLIDE

Oklahoma looked like it didn't know what hit it throughout trouncing

By Glenn Guilbeau

For 3 minutes and 10 seconds in the first quarter Saturday at Mercedes-Benz Stadium, No. 4 Oklahoma was tied 7-7 with No. 1 LSU.

This was new ground for the Tigers, who had not trailed in a game since Auburn took a 13-10 lead early in the third quarter on Oct. 26 before succumbing and falling behind, 23-13, in a 23-20 loss. No one had been even with LSU other than 0-0 since Auburn and LSU were at 10-10 at halftime of that game.

But there it was on the scoreboard with 7:34 to go in the first period — Oklahoma 7, LSU 7.

And then in a flash, Oklahoma was done and buried by Burrow.

The Tigers scored touchdowns on their next six possessions to close the first half and take a 49-14 lead before winning the Peach Bowl national semifinal, 63-28, in front of 78,347.

"What can you say? We traded blows early," an exasperated Oklahoma coach Lincoln Riley said. "They went on the run there at the end of the first half."

Actually, the run started at the end of the first quarter, but Riley was spinning for most of the game.

"We got a little frantic," Riley said.

This is understandable.

The Tigers continued their run on their first possession of the third quarter to take a 56-14 lead, begin making travel plans for New Orleans, and rest their starters.

LSU tight end Thaddeus Moss leaps over Oklahoma Sooners safety Pat Fields during the first quarter of the dominant Peach Bowl win. (Jason Getz/USA TODAY Sports)

LSU, 14-0 for the first time in program history, advances to the national championship game on Jan. 13 at 7 p.m. in the Mercedes-Benz Superdome in New Orleans to play No. 3 Clemson (14-0), which beat No. 2 Ohio State, 29-23, in the other national semifinal Saturday night at the Fiesta Bowl.

Oklahoma's secondary was as frantic as Riley's sideline, often arriving later — rather than sooner — as LSU quarterback Joe Burrow threw seven touchdown passes and completed 21-of-27 passes for 403 yards in the first half alone.

"They kept their foot on the pedal, and we took some plays off out there," Oklahoma cornerback Parnell Motley admitted. "They have a great offense. It's more than I expected — more live in person."

Burrow finished early in the fourth quarter with 29 completions in 39 attempts for a career-high 493 yards that is second in LSU history behind Rohan Davey's 528 against Alabama in 2001. Burrow's seven touchdown passes broke the LSU record of six set by him at Vanderbilt this season.

The seven touchdown passes also shattered the previous New Year's Day Six Bowl (Rose, Sugar, Orange, Cotton, Fiesta, and Peach) record of five and the national semifinal and Peach Bowl records of four. Burrow also tied the record for most touchdown passes in any bowl's history.

But in his words, he had an off day.

"To be honest, it wasn't my sharpest game," he said and added that wide receiver Justin Jefferson was "bailing me out on a couple throws that I had missed."

Jefferson caught 14 passes for 227 yards and four touchdowns — the most in the history of the Peach Bowl, New Year's Day Six bowls, and national semifinals.

When Burrow scored on a 3-yard run for a 56-14 lead with 10:11 to play in the third quarter, he became the first player in upper level college football history to account for eight touchdowns in a bowl game of any kind.

Tigers wide receiver Justin Jefferson stretches for a touchdown ahead of Oklahoma safety Pat Fields during the first quarter of the 63-28 win. (Dale Zanine/USA TODAY Sports)

LSU
7
ESPN

Oklahoma graduate transfer quarterback Jalen Hurts, meanwhile, managed to complete just 5-of-18 passes for 27 percent in the first half for 101 yards with an interception. This from a quarterback who entered the game No. 3 in the nation in efficiency at 200.3 on 222-of-309 passing for 71 percent and 3,634 yards and 32 touchdowns. He also came in averaging 96 yards rushing a game, but managed just 24 on eight carries in the first half amid two sacks.

With the game long decided, Hurts was able to pad his stats and finished 15-of-31 passing for 217 yards and zero touchdowns with 43 yards on 14 carries in his final college performance.

Hurts didn't quite recognize this LSU team. He had beat the Tigers of a different time twice as Alabama's starting quarterback in 2016 and '17 by scores of 10-0 and 24-10 and watched as new starting quarterback Tua Tagovailoa was part of a 29-0 win in 2018 at Tiger Stadium.

That was the game that motivated Orgeron to go to the spread offense full throttle and to hire Joe Brady, an offensive assistant with the Saints, to be his pass game coordinator.

"I think the obvious difference is they're scoring 50-something points," Hurts deadpanned. "They have a hell of an offense."

In LSU's last national championship game appearance, it did not have close to that and lost, 21-0, to Alabama in the Superdome on Jan. 9, 2012, as the purple-and-gold crowd never quite got into it.

The Tigers figure they will not be shut out this time.

"We go into every game thinking no one can stop us," Burrow said.

"Obviously, it's going to be a great day," Orgeron said of Jan. 13, 2020. "The state of Louisiana is going to be on fire." ■

Head coach Ed Orgeron celebrates with safety Grant Delpit (7) and wide receiver Justin Jefferson (2) after defeating the Oklahoma Sooners and advancing to the national championship game. (Brett Davis/USA TODAY Sports)

Joe Burrow reacts after being named offensive MVP of the 2019 Peach Bowl, another accolade in his unforgettable season. (Brett Davis/ USA TODAY Sports)